The Rise and Fall
of Imperial Japan

The Rise and Fall
of Imperial Japan

Stephen Wynn

PEN & SWORD
HISTORY

AN IMPRINT OF PEN & SWORD BOOKS LTD.
YORKSHIRE – PHILADELPHIA

First published in Great Britain in 2020 by
Pen & Sword Military
An imprint of
Pen & Sword Books Ltd
Yorkshire – Philadelphia

ISBN 978 1 47383 5 788

A CIP catalogue record for this book is
available from the British Library.

Printed and bound in England by TJ International, Padstow, Cornwall

Pen & Sword Books Limited incorporates the imprints of Atlas, Archaeology,
Aviation, Discovery, Family History, Fiction, History, Maritime, Military,
Military Classics, Politics, Select, Transport, True Crime, Air World,
Frontline Publishing, Leo Cooper, Remember When, Seaforth Publishing,
The Praetorian Press, Wharncliffe Local History, Wharncliffe Transport,
Wharncliffe True Crime and White Owl.

For a complete list of Pen & Sword titles please contact

PEN & SWORD BOOKS LIMITED
47 Church Street, Barnsley, South Yorkshire, S70 2AS, England
E-mail: enquiries@pen-and-sword.co.uk
Website: www.pen-and-sword.co.uk

Or

PEN AND SWORD BOOKS
1950 Lawrence Rd, Havertown, PA 19083, USA
E-mail: Uspen-and-sword@casematepublishers.com
Website: www.penandswordbooks.com

Contents

How does a once great Empire like Japan lose it all? Was it naivety, greed, arrogance, poor leadership, economics, political interference, military defeat, or maybe a combination of some or all of these factors?

The leader of the first ever Japanese Empire was the Emperor Jimmu. According to legend, Jimmu was born on 13 February, which is the first day of the first month of the Chinese calendar, in 711 BCE, and died on 9 April 585. He reigned for seventy-five years. According to Japanese mythology he was a descendant of the sun goddess Amaterasu through her grandson Ninigi and of the storm God Susanoo.

Emperor Jimmu decided to set out on a military expedition which began at Hyuga, an old Japanese province on the east coast of Kyushu near the Seto Inland Sea which separates Honshu, Shikoku, and Kyushu, three of the four main islands of Japan. Going on to capture Yamato in Fukuoka, he made this the centre of his power. Yamato became the name given to the whole of Japan and this period of history is known as the Yamato period.

CHAPTER ONE

The Emperor Meiji

Prince Mutsuhito was the son of the Emperor Komei and one of his concubines, Nakayama Yoshiko, a lady in waiting in the court of the Imperial House of Japan. At birth he was given the name Prince Sachi, or Sachinomiya. Meiji was the 122nd emperor of Japan and came to power on 3 February 1867, the first day of the Imperial Japanese Empire which lasted until 1947.

When he was 7, on 16 August 1860, he was proclaimed prince of the blood and heir to his father's throne. On the same day he was formally adopted by his father's consort, Empress Dowager Eisho. A year later he became the Crown Prince and was given the adult name of Mutsuhito.

In 1853 Commodore Matthew Perry of the American Navy arrived in Tokyo harbour, which at the time was known as Edo, with a squadron of ships. The purpose of Perry's mission was to open up trade links between Japan and America. This caused much debate in Japan, and for the first time in 250 years the Shogunate made contact with the Imperial Court to consult with them about what should be done. Perry had not made a polite request in his desire to begin a trade agreement, instead he warned the Japanese that there would be military consequences if they did not agree. Japanese forces were no match for the Americans. Emperor Komei's officials felt that they should agree to Perry's request. Accordingly the Japanese agreed to trade with the Americans and even submitted to what were known as 'Unequal Treaties', which meant giving up tariff authority and the right to try foreigners in its courts.

By the early 1860s the Japanese way of life and the very structure of its society was also under threat by internal conflict. This was because the main beneficiaries of international trade were the Shogunate, which displeased the Daimyos. With so much money being made from this trade, and more foreign governments seeking similar agreements, groups of Shishi (young samurai), supporters of the Emperor Komei, were all for direct acts of violence, against both the Shogunate and foreigners, favouring their expulsion from the country.

Rather than uniting with the shishi and the Emperor so that they could all benefit from trade, the Shogunate did their best to divide the factions so that they remained in overall control of foreign trade. But the shishi had sufficient sway with the Emperor to persuade him to issue an 'Order to expel barbarians', which he happily did on 11 March 1863. Foreigners were given two months to leave: the final day was 11 May.

For the Shogunate, this was a problem: for them, more foreigners meant more money. When the deadline came, attacks began against the Shogunate as well as foreigners. Rebels fired on foreign ships in the waters of the Shimonoseki Strait, the waterway that separates the islands of Honshu and Kyushu. There was no sanctuary on land either. The *ronin*, masterless samurai, joined the fight and killed a number of westerners and Shogunate officials.

One of the westerners killed at this time was English merchant Charles Lennox Richardson, who had lived and traded in Shanghai since 1853. In September 1862, having made his fortune, Richardson decided to retire and return to England a wealthy man. On his way home, the ship he was on stopped off at the Japanese port of Yokohama. There he met a friend from Shanghai, a gentleman by the name of Woodthorpe Charles Clarke. They in turn met up with a fellow English merchant named William Marshall and his sister-in-law Margaret Watson Borradaile. Together they went on a sight-seeing tour on horseback, with their final destination being the 700-year-old Buddhist temple in Kawasaki Daishi, some twenty kilometres from Tokyo. As the four travelled through the village of Namamugi, they came across the Satsuma regent, Shimazu Hisamitsu, and his entourage, travelling in the opposite direction. An altercation of some description took place between the two groups which resulted in Richardson being killed and both Clarke and Marshall being wounded. At the inquest into Richardson's death, Clarke and Marshall stated that as they were travelling through Namamugi they saw a group of samurai ahead of them but did not realise that they were part of a daimyo party. As they turned a corner they suddenly realised they were 'twelve men deep into the procession and close to the daimyo'. But as they had not been shouted at or challenged by the samurai, they were confident that they would not be hostile towards them. But as they attempted to turn their horses, one of the samurai struck Richardson a blow with his sword, and then did the same to Marshall. Fearing for their lives the men reared up their horses and ran, receiving more wounds as they went. Richardson died later of his wounds.

Fifteen years later an account from the Satsuma concerning the incident surfaced in the form of a pamphlet, written by American journalist E.H. House. It stated that Richardson was 'notorious for his violent dealings with the Chinese while he had lived in Shanghai'. Different accounts of Richardson described him as being 'reckless, stubborn, and arrogant'. All include the sentence, 'Mr Charles Lennox Richardson, of Shanghai… was murdered in cold blood.'

When he was 14, Crown Prince Mutsuhito was studying classical poetry. At the same time, Prince Tokugawa Yoshinobu, became the 15th and final Shogun. He was something of a visionary and a reformer who wanted to transform Japan in to a Western style nation, but not all of those around him agreed and he met with a degree of resistance.

In January 1867, Emperor Komei became unwell and after a short illness he died. Three days later, in a brief ceremony in Kyoto, the Crown Prince ascended to the 'Chrysanthemum Throne' and was sworn in as the next Emperor of Japan. Despite his new status, Mutsuhito did not concern himself in political matters but continued with his classical studies.

At the same time the new Shogun, Tokugawa Yoshinobu, struggled to keep the old ways together, and control over his subordinates. An agreement was reached which saw Yoshinobu lose his law-making powers but keep his title as Shogun, but on 9 November 1867, with the agreement having broken down, he resigned, officially tendering his resignation to the Emperor, and formally stepped down ten days later.

On 4 January 1868, the Emperor read out a document before the Imperial court, proclaiming the restoration of Imperial rule:

> *The Emperor of Japan announces to the sovereigns of all foreign countries and to their subjects that permission has been granted to the shogun, Tokugawa Yoshinobu, to return the governing power in accordance with his own request. We shall henceforward exercise supreme authority in all the internal and external affairs of the country. Consequently, the title of Emperor must be substituted for that of Tycoon, in which the treaties have been made. Officers are being appointed by us to the conduct of foreign affairs. It is desirable that the representatives of the treaty powers recognise this announcement.*
>
> *Mutsuhito.*

The Charter Oath was presented to the Emperor on 7 April 1868, which in essence was a five-part statement of the intentions and the direction which the country would follow during the Emperor's reign. It set out the legal stage for Japan's modernisation, and it changed the structure of society by freeing peoples of all classes to change their jobs, so people from the countryside were free to look for work in the city, where they could obtain better jobs and more pay.

The oath consisted of five clauses:

1. *Deliberative assemblies shall be widely established and all matters decided by open discussion.*
2. *All classes, high and low, shall be united in vigorously carrying out the administration of affairs of state.*
3. *The common people, no less than the civil and military officials, shall all be allowed to pursue their own calling so that there may be no discontent.*
4. *Evil customs of the past shall be broken off and everything based upon the laws of nature.*
5. *Knowledge shall be sought throughout the world so as to strengthen the foundation of the Imperial rule.*

The final draft was not the original one. It had been written by Yuri Kimimasa, a senior councillor of the Imperial Court who dealt with the financial and monetary policy of the Meiji government, but was then toned down to make it sound less alarming. The final draft was written by Kido Takayoshi, a nobleman and a statesman of the Meiji Restoration.

The oath was read out in the ceremonial hall of the Kyoto Imperial Palace in the presence of the Emperor and some 400 officials of the Imperial Court and the government. They praised the oath and swore to uphold and implement it. Eventually the document contained 767 signatures.

Shogun Yoshinobu resisted pro-Imperial forces briefly, but by the end of 1869 the last of the 'bakufu' strongholds had been defeated, and in September 1870 the era was officially changed to Meiji, which in English means 'enlightened rule'. It also became the Emperor's name after his death, which marked the start of the custom of posthumously naming the Emperor after the name of the era during which they ruled.

It is he who was largely responsible for turning Japan into one of the world's great powers. At the time of his birth in 1852, the country was a feudal-dominated system which had been in place for centuries, split into more than 250 domains, each controlled by a warrior and his men. Collectively these were controlled by the Tokugawa Shogunate, which was a feudal military government, with the head being the Shogun. The Shogun in fact wielded more power than the Emperor did. Under them came the *daimyo* or feudal lords, who were also wealthy and powerful individuals.

Emperor Meiji had the vision and desire to transform Japan in to an industrialised nation and a major power on the world stage.

Sometime in May 1868, for the first time since his early childhood, the Emperor left the safety of his imperial home in Kyoto to take charge of his forces which were seeking out what was left of the bakufu armies. Because of the large crowds that had turned out to get a glimpse of their Emperor, it took him three days to travel from Kyoto and Osaka, a distance of 26 miles. His purpose wasn't military, it was so that he could be seen by as many of his people and foreign envoys as possible. When he returned home, it was announced that he would take charge of state affairs, and that any further studies that he undertook would be done in his leisure time. From 1871 onwards he was educated in state affairs. He attended cabinet meetings and other government functions. His style was more to observe than to speak, although he did occasionally.

On 19 September 1868 the Emperor announced that the city of Edo was to have its name changed to Tokyo, which means 'eastern capital', and embarked on a journey there by road, the first time he had been to the city. In Tokyo he visited the harbour, where he boarded a Japanese naval vessel for the first time. The next day he gave instructions that research should be carried out to see how best Japan's navy could be strengthened and improved.

Meanwhile, the rebel forces who had supported the Emperor and had helped defeat the armies of the Shogunate, had formed themselves into a Council of State. From them, three were selected to lead the government. By 1885 this method had progressed to become a system based on a western European style of government, where a Prime Minister would lead a cabinet of politicians.

In 1871, Emperor Meiji announced an end to 'domains', which were abolished and replaced with 'prefectures' which were the first level of control beneath the Council of State. The end of the domains also saw an end to the daimyos. They were compensated with an annual salary of one tenth of what they had previously earned, on condition that they moved to Tokyo. Most took the decision to retire from politics rather than move.

The biggest losers of all of these changes were the samurai, who lost many of their traditional privileges, including their payments from the government, which for many left them with no way of supporting themselves and their families.

In the Sakuradamon Incident of 24 March 1860, on the day of the Double Third Festival where all of the daimyos who were stationed in Edo (Tokyo) were scheduled to enter Edo Castle for meetings, one Li had just arrived at the castle. He was by the Sakurado Gate with an entourage of some sixty samurai guards. Li was being carried in a palanquin with a samurai from the Satsuma Domain named Arimura Jisaemon, when an attack at the front of Li's entourage drew everybody's attention, leaving a lone gunman to fire one shot in to the palanquin wounding Li in the process. Arimura helped Li out of the palanquin, laid him on the ground and decapitated him with one strike of his sword, before performing the Japanese ritual suicide of seppuku.

In the Satsuma Rebellion of 1877, disaffected samurai revolted against the imperial government, despite the fact that the Satsuma domain had more than played its part in the Meiji Restoration. The fighting continued until 24 September, finally ending in the Battle of Shiroyama. By then there were only forty rebel samurai left, and they carried out a full frontal assault on the Imperial forces. The outcome was the death of the rebel leader, Saigo Takamori, and all of his men. Takimori was one of the most influential samurai in Japanese history, and has often been called the last true samurai.

Despite the changes and upheavals of Emperor Meiji's reign, he did bring stability. He had ruled for 45 years. The Meiji Restoration is spoken of favourably by the Japanese people. It was after all the foundation of their lives to this day in many ways. During his reign Japan greatly increased her industrial output to such a degree that she became a major power on the world stage and the most influential nation in the Pacific, though it is debateable how much of a part the Emperor personally played in the Restoration.

There was an attempt to assassinate Emperor Meiji on 20 May 1910. This was known as the High Treason Incident. When police searched the room of Miyashita Takichi, who worked at a lumber mill in the Nangano Prefecture, they found bomb making materials. Further enquiries led to the police arresting a further five individuals, Nitta Toru, Niimura Tadao, Furukawa Rikisaku, Kotoku Shusui and his former common-law wife and feminist author Kanno Suga. After questioning them, the authorities determined that there was a nationwide conspiracy by 'socialist anarchists' against the Emperor and his family. More arrests following and by the time the matter had been fully investigated, twenty-five men and one woman had been charged, four of whom were Buddhist monks. They were tried in camera on 18 January 1911, no press were allowed in. Despite most of the evidence being circumstantial, 24 out of the 26 defendants were found guilty, 11 of whom were hanged. They included Uchiyama Gudo, one of the Buddhist monks, Shusui, a prominent Japanese anarchist, Oishi Seinosuke, a doctor, and the only female in the group, Kanno. The whole incident appears to have been an excuse for the authorities to round up those they expected of being dissidents. Already some of the country's more prominent activists were in prison, having been arrested in what was known as the Red Flag Incident of 22 June 1908, which had marked a turning point in how the Japanese government dealt with the issue of socialism. They became determined to stamp it out once and for all.

The following is a time-line of landmarks of the Meiji era:

1852:	Birth of Emperor Meiji.
1853:	8 July, American ships under Commodore Matthew Perry arrive in Japan demanding a trade agreement.
1854/5:	Treaties signed by the Shogunate and the Americans.
1850s-60s:	The Sonno joi movement is at its peak. Sonno joi was a Sino-Japanese political philosophy and social movement derived from Neo-Confucianism, and was part of the movement that attempted to overthrow the Tokugawa Shogunate.
1858:	The Shogunate signs treaties with Holland, Russia, and Great Britain. Cholera outbreak ravages Japan 1858-60.
1860:	24 March, assassination of the Chief Minister Tairo Ii Nasouke by ronin, samurai of the Mito Domain, in the Sakuradamon Incident. 11 November, Sachinomiya is formally proclaimed Crown Prince and given the personal name of Mutsuhito.
1862:	14 September, the Namamugi Incident was an assault on British subjects by an armed retinue of Shimazu Hisamitsu in Japan. It occurred just six days after Sir Ernest Mason Satow, a British diplomat, set foot on Japanese soil.

1864-55:   Bombardment of Shimonoseki by British, American, French and Dutch naval vessels.

1867:   31 January, death of Emperor Komei from smallpox. Accession to the throne of Mutsuhito.

1868:   4 January, the end of 265 years of rule by the Tokugawa Shogunate, and the formal restoration of Imperial rule.
12 September, formal enthronement of the Emperor.
23 October, name of the era changed to Meiji.
6 November, the capital of Japan is moved from Kyoto to Edo and renamed Tokyo.

1869:   11 January, the Emperor marries Ichijo Haruko, who becomes the Empress Shoken.
4 September, the Emperor receives the Duke of Edinburgh.

1860s-1881: A period of rebellion and assassination in Japan.

1871:   The abolition of the Han system announced, replaced by a system of prefectures – the culmination of the Meiji Restoration.

1872:   5 November, the Emperor receives Grand Duke Alexei Alexandrovich of Russia.

1873:   Edo Castle is destroyed by fire. The Emperor moves to the Akasaka Palace in Tokyo.

1877:   The Satsuma Rebellion – a revolt of disaffected samurai against the imperial government.

1879:   31 August, birth of Prince Yoshihito who would go on to become the Emperor Taisho, the Emperor's only surviving son.

1881:   The Emperor receives the first state visit of a foreign monarch, King Kalakaua from Hawaii.

1885:   22 December, Ito Hirobumi becomes the first Prime Minister of Japan.

1889:   11 February, proclamation of the constitution of the Empire of Japan.

1894-5:   The Sino-Japanese War. China pays reparations to Japan, Korea receives independence.

1901:   Emperor Meiji becomes a grandfather with the birth of the future Emperor, Showa.

1904-5:   8 February, beginning of the Russo-Japanese War. Japan's comprehensive victory over Russia came as a complete shock to other world powers.

1910:   22 August, annexation of Korea by the Empire of Japan.

1912:   30 July, Emperor Meiji dies.

CHAPTER TWO

Wars and Conflicts

This chapter takes a very brief look at the wars and conflicts in which Japan was involved during the existence of the Imperial Japanese Empire.

Boshin War 1868-9. I have written about this in another chapter.

Japanese invasion of Taiwan 1874. Although China claimed the Ryukyu Islands, Japan annexed them in 1872. A ship from the Ryukyu Islands was wrecked in inclement weather near the southern tip of Taiwan, and 54 members of the crew of 66 were beheaded by the local aborigines. They took the twelve remaining crewmen to Tainan in southern Taiwan. The local Qing Chinese government then took them to Fujian in mainland China, from where the Qing government sent them back home.

The Japanese authorities were not pleased and sought compensation from the Chinese government, a claim that was rejected as China said that the natives of Taiwan were outside their jurisdiction. The Meiji government then asked the leaders of the Taiwanese aborigines to punish those responsible for the murders but they were given the same response.

On 6 May 1872 a small force of Japanese soldiers led by former United States Union Navy veteran, Douglas Cassel, landed on the southern tip of Taiwan and made camp. Some days later Cassel met with the head of the island's sixteen tribes, Chief Issa. He told Cassel that the 'Botan tribe' were out of his control.

On 17 May a patrol of one hundred Japanese soldiers made their way inland to look for another location to set up camp. On the way they were ambushed and attacked by a group of Botans. A Japanese sergeant was killed and one soldier wounded. Initially the body of the dead sergeant was left where he fell, but the Japanese later returned to collect the body only to discover that his head had been cut off and taken away.

In another patrol on 21 May, two more Japanese soldiers were seriously wounded when they were once again ambushed by members of the Botan tribe. Japanese reinforcements were brought in the next day and a further engagement took place in which a Japanese officer and five soldiers were killed and thirty were wounded.

The Japanese remained in Taiwan until 1874. They withdrew after the Chinese government agreed to pay them 18.7 tons of silver.

South Western War 1877. This, which I have written about in the previous chapter, was also known as the Satsuma Rebellion. It was a revolt by a group of samurai warriors disaffected with the new Imperial Meiji government. The rebellion lasted from 29 January to 24 September 1877 and resulted in a victory for the

Imperial forces, but not before 15,000 of their men were killed and 7,000 wounded. As for the samurai, they had 10,000 of their men killed, 11,000 wounded, and 4,000 either surrendered or deserted.

First Sino-Japanese War 1894-5. This was the first overseas war Japan had been involved in since she came out of enforced isolation in the 1860s. A new look and modernised Japanese army inflicted a somewhat unexpected and embarrassing defeat on Chinese forces.

Japanese Invasion of Taiwan 1895. This was a conflict between the Empire of Japan and the armed forces of the short-lived Republic of Formosa, after the Qing dynasty of China had ceded Taiwan to Japan in April 1895 at the end of the First Sino-Japanese War.

The occupation of Taiwan by the Japanese lasted from 29 May until 21 October 1895. Initially the Japanese sent 7,000 troops to Taiwan. By the time they left that number had risen to 37,000. Twelve warships of the Imperial Japanese Navy were stationed there. Taiwanese losses during this brief occupation were approximately 14,000, which included civilians. The Japanese lost 164 men killed in combat and 515 wounded, but their greatest enemy was disease, mostly cholera and malaria, which killed 4,642. This number included Prince Kitashirakawa Yoshihisa. Among the Taiwanese dead were a number of Hakka peasants, allegedly murdered by Japanese soldiers in revenge for the killing of Japanese teachers in Taipei.

Boxer Rebellion 1899-1901. The Boxer Rebellion was an anti-imperialist, anti-foreign and anti-Christian uprising that took place in China between 1899 and 1901. It was initiated by the Militia United in Righteousness known in English as the 'Boxers'. Many of their members had practiced martial arts. The uprising took place against a background of drought and disruption brought on in the main by the growth of foreign influence in China. After months of increasing levels of violence in Shandong and other parts of China in June 1900, a number of Boxers, convinced they were invulnerable to foreign weapons, arrived in Beijing chanting the slogan 'Support the Qing government and exterminate foreigners.' Both foreigners and Chinese Christians had to seek refuge in the Beijing Legation Quarter.

A coalition force from eight nations – America, Austria-Hungary, Britain, France, Germany, Italy, Japan and Russia – arrived in China to lift the siege. The initially hesitant Empress Dowager Cixi eventually supported the Boxers and on 21 June she issued an imperial decree declaring war on these eight nations. Diplomats, foreign civilians, soldiers, as well as Chinese Christians holed up in the Legation Quarter were under siege for fifty-five days by the Imperial Army of China and the Boxers. Chinese officials were split on the issue of who supported the Boxers and who favoured conciliation. The latter group were led by Prince Qing. The supreme commander of the Chinese forces, Manchu General Ronglu later claimed that he acted to protect the foreigners, and some elements of the Chinese Army refused the imperial order to fight against foreigners.

The coalition forces brought 20,000 troops to China, defeated the Imperial Chinese Army, and arrived in Peking on August 14 and relieved those under siege in the Legation Quarter. This in turn led to the capital being plundered, along with the surrounding countryside. Those who were suspected of being Boxer rebels faced summary execution, and the Boxer Protocol of 7 September 1901 provided for the execution of government officials who had supported the Boxers. The protocol also determined that foreign troops were to be stationed in Beijing, and $10 billion (2018 value) was to be paid as an indemnity over the next thirty-nine years to the eight nations involved.

Russo-Japanese War 8 February 1904 to 5 September 1905. This has gone down in history as the first great war of the twentieth century. It started, as many wars do, out of greed, a desire to take control of another region. On this occasion it was because the Russian Empire and the Imperial Japanese Empire both had designs over Manchuria and Korea. Russia sought a warm-water port on the Pacific Ocean. Discussions between Russia and Japan broke down and the countries ended up at war with one another. After a number of sea and land battles, Japan were victorious, which greatly surprised the nations of the world. All of a sudden, Japan had arrived on the world stage as a major power.

Beipu Uprising November 1907. This was the first of several armed local uprisings against the Japanese forces occupying the island of Taiwan. It was in response to the oppression of the indigenous population by the Japanese authorities. A number of insurgents from the Hakka, a subgroup of the Han Chinese and Saisiyat, in what is today Beipu, attacked Japanese officials and their families. Japanese retaliation was swift and bloody. The Japanese military and police murdered over a hundred of the Hakka people.

Truku War 1914. The Truku War was another case of an indigenous race of Chinese people on Taiwan rising up against their treatment by the occupying Japanese.

The Truku occupied a large area of land over which the Japanese wanted to have control. The fighting began in May and continued on and off until August when the Japanese secured a victory over the Truku people.

Tapani Incident 1915. This was one of the largest armed uprisings by Taiwanese Han and aboriginals against Japanese rule in Taiwan. The incident started at the Xilai Temple in Tainan and resulted in Japanese police stations being stormed by armed Han fighters.

It was interesting how both sides viewed events: the Taiwanese talked of 'fighting for their independence' or as being 'nationalists', while the Japanese referred to the incident as being 'a large scale instance of banditry led by criminal elements'.

Russian Civil War 1917-22. During the Russian Civil War the Japanese sent troops to Siberia as part of a much larger effort by a number of western nations, to help white Russian forces in their fight against the Bolshevik Red Army. The Japanese had 1,399 of their men killed, with a further 1,717 dying from sickness. Japan claimed to be in Siberia to safeguard stockpiled military supplies and to rescue the Czechoslovak Legion. But their real reasons were more likely anti-communist sentiment, a desire to reclaim territory lost in the past, and outright territorial acquisition. Anyway, as is well known, the Red Army were eventually victorious.

After the war Japan's army and government were involved in a bitter controversy. The official conduct of the Siberian Intervention was attacked in the Japanese Diet, with the army being accused of grossly misrepresenting the size of the forces sent, misappropriating secret funds. Their support of figures such as Baron von Ungern-Sternberg of the White Army, rumours of whose grotesque atrocities had reached the Japanese newspapers, were ill-judged.

Wushe Rebellion 1930. Also known as the Musha Incident, the Wushe Rebellion was the last major uprising against occupying Japanese forces in Taiwan. Once again it occurred because of long-term oppression by the Japanese authorities. The Seediq indigenous group attacked a village killing over 130 Japanese. In response, the Japanese led a relentless counter-attack, killing over 600 Seediq. The handling of the incident by the Japanese authorities was strongly criticised, leading to many changes in aboriginal policy.

March incident 1931. This was an abortive coup by a number of army officers of the Imperial Japanese Army. Those involved were members of the radical Sakurakai (Cherry) secret society, helped by a number of civilians from ultranationalist groups. The same group tried twice in the same year, with the exact same outcome.

The Sakurakai had been founded in the autumn of 1930 by Lieutenant Colonel Kingoro Hashimoto and Captain Isamu Cho. In Japanese culture, the cherry blossom was the symbol of self-sacrifice and symbolised a soldier's potentially fleeting life.

Japanese invasion of Manchuria 1931-2. Manchuria was invaded by the Kwantung army of the Empire of Japan immediately following the Mukden Incident (see later). The Japanese established a puppet state which they called Manchukuo which lasted until the end of the Second World War.

In violation of orders from Tokyo, the commander in chief of the Kwantung army, General Shigeru Honjo, ordered his forces to move quickly to expand operations all along the line of the South Manchurian Railway. Troops duly moved along the railway line and captured virtually every city on a 730-mile front in a few days.

Also on 19 September, the Chosun Army in Korea departed for Manchuria without authorization from the Emperor.

Between 20 and 25 September, Japanese forces took several other cities, securing control of Liaoning and Kirin provinces and the main line of rail communications to Korea.

But the news of these victories was met not with celebrations in Tokyo but shock, because the army had acted without orders from the central government. The Japanese civilian government was thrown into disarray by this massive act of insubordination, but as reports of one quick victory after another began to pour in, it was powerless to oppose the army. In fact it was decided to send three more infantry divisions from Japan.

During this era, the elected Japanese government could be held hostage by the army and navy, since they were constitutionally necessary for the formation of cabinets. Without their support, the government would not survive very long.

January 28 Incident, 1932. On 18 January five Japanese Buddhist monks, members of an ardently nationalist sect, were beaten near Shanghai's Sanyou Factory by agitated Chinese civilians. Two were seriously injured and one later died. But that wasn't the end of the matter, the group were not satisfied and continued their rampage by burning down the factory.

When the local police arrived to deal with the disorder, one was killed and several more were hurt. The police presence caused more problems with anti-Japanese and anti-imperialist protestors in the city. Chinese residents of Shanghai marched in the streets calling for a boycott of Japanese-made goods.

Over the following week the situation continued to deteriorate, and by 27 January the Japanese military had concentrated thirty ships, forty aircraft and 7,000 troops around the shoreline of Shanghai to put down any resistance in the event that further violence broke out. The military justified its actions by saying that it had to defend its concession and its citizens.

The Japanese issued an ultimatum to the Shanghai Municipal Council in which they demanded public condemnation for any damage that had been caused in the aftermath of the incident with the monks, monetary compensation by the Chinese community, and that the Chinese government take steps to suppress further anti-Japanese protests. They agreed to these demands.

Meanwhile the Chinese 19th Route Army, who were really nothing more than a criminal gang, had been growing in strength just outside the city. Shanghai's authorities offered them a large sum of money to leave them alone.

At midnight on 28 January Japanese aircraft, having taken off from an aircraft-carrier, began bombing. Soon after, 3,000 troops of the Imperial Japanese Army attacked prearranged targets within the city, including the North Railway station. The 19th Route Army accepted the larger sum of money, but didn't leave their base on the outskirts of the city. Instead they stayed to help defend the city and fight against the Japanese, putting up a fierce resistance.

The capital of China at the time was Nanking, sometimes written Nanjing. It was close enough to Shanghai for there to be major concern for its safety. On 30 January, Chiang Kai-shek, leader of the Republic of China, decided that it was best to move the Chinese capital to Luoyang.

Shanghai had many foreign interests invested in it, so the US, the UK and France all tried to negotiate a ceasefire between Japan and China. Japan refused to co-operate, and continued to mobilise its troops, although on 12 February they accepted a half-day cease-fire for civilian relief. Later that day, the Japanese demanded that the Chinese Army retreat 20 km from the border of the Shanghai concessions, a demand which the Chinese promptly rejected. Subsequently, the number of Japanese troops was increased to 90,000, supported by 80 warships and 300 aeroplanes.

On 5 May a peace was agreed with the help of the League of Nations and Shanghai became a demilitarised zone.

May 15 Incident 1932. This was an attempted coup d'état by conservative elements within the Navy, aided by cadets and civilian members of the ultra-nationalist League of Blood. The Japanese Prime Minister, Inukai Tsuyoshi, was assassinated by eleven young naval officers. In the subsequent trial the support of the Japanese population led to extremely light sentences for those who murdered the Prime Minister, strengthening the Japanese military and a weakening democracy and the rule of law in the Empire of Japan.

Soviet-Japanese border conflicts 1932-9. Also known as the Soviet-Japanese Border War, this was an undeclared conflict fought between the Soviet Union and Japan. As Japan extended her control over China, she headed towards the north-east of the country, getting ever closer to the border with the Soviet Union, which led to growing tensions between the two nations. Both sides regularly violated the border, which resulted in numerous skirmishes. These continued on and off until the Battle of Khalkhin Gol in 1939, when a joint Soviet and Mongolian force finally defeated the Japanese forces and returned the border region to stability.

Actions in Inner Mongolia 1933-6. This was part of the ongoing campaign by the Empire of Japan to invade Northern China before the official start to the Second Sino-Japanese War. In 1931, the invasion of Manchuria secured the creation of the puppet state of Manchukuo, and in 1933 Operation Nekka separated the province of Jehol from the Republic of China. Finding its way blocked to the south by the Tanggu Truce, the Imperial Japanese Army decided to head west towards the Inner Mongolian provinces of Chahar and Suiyuan with the aim of establishing a northern China buffer state. To avoid overt violations of the truce, the Japanese government used proxy armies in these campaigns while Chinese resistance was at first only provided by anti-Japanese resistance movement forces in Chahar.

Chinese government forces resisted Japanese aggression only in Suivuan in 1936, possibly because they did not wish to antagonise the Japanese.

Military Academy Incident 1934. A group of five cadets from the Imperial Japanese Army Academy, led by two officers who belonged to the radical militarist Imperial Way Faction at the academy were troubled by the perceived loss of influence of their faction over the military following the dismissal of Army Minister Sadao Araki in January 1934. They came up with a plan for overthrowing the government. However, in early November 1934, Sato, one of the cadets, betrayed his colleagues and informed the government about the plan and the Faction.

Forewarned of this betrayal, Captain Tsuji Masanobu, the company commander at the Army Academy, arranged the arrest of the principals by the Kempeitai, or secret police, on 20 November 1934. Because of a lack of any real evidence, the accused could not be charged or convicted of any offences; but the five cadets were all expelled from the Academy. The two officers were suspended for six months.

February 26 Incident, 1936. This was a failed coup d'état by junior officers of the Imperial Japanese Army.

Second Sino-Japanese War 7 July 1937 to 2 September 1945. This began with the 'Marco Polo Bridge Incident' of 1937 in which a dispute between Japanese and Chinese troops escalated into a full-scale war. China managed to sustain her fight against Japan with aid from both the Soviet Union and the United States.

The Second Sino-Japanese War was the largest Asian war of the twentieth century. It accounted for most of the civilian and military casualties in the Pacific War, with between 10 and 25 million Chinese civilians and over 4 million Chinese and Japanese military personnel dying from war-related violence, famine, and other causes.

Second World War 1939-45. This, of course, was a step too far for the Imperial Japanese Empire and was its final downfall.

CHAPTER THREE

The Imperial Japanese Army

The Imperial Japanese Army, founded in 1871, in theory came under the command of the Emperor but in reality was controlled by the Ministry of War and the Office of the General Staff. It ceased to exist with Japan's surrender at the Second World War. On the outbreak of the Second World War and the Japanese attack on Pearl Harbor on 7 December 1941 which brought America into the war, the Imperial Japanese Army had 1.7 million men serving in 51 divisions. This included 27 divisions stationed in China as an army of occupation and 13 divisions in defensive positions along the border with Mongolia.

By 1945, Japan had increased the number of men it had in its armed forces to five million. Soldiers of the Imperial Japanese Army had a reputation for being dedicated, fearless and fanatical fighters, who were prepared to give their lives for their Emperor. For Japanese soldiers, honour was everything. To be captured and taken as a prisoner of war brought shame to the soldier and his family. So for a Japanese soldier who didn't want to be taken prisoner, there were three options: stay and fight to the last man, a 'banzai' charge with bayonets drawn, or suicide by 'hari-kiri' or with a grenade.

The training of Japanese soldiers was harsh, with insufficient food, over-strenuous duties and beatings. Some argue that this, combined with the Japanese contempt for soldiers who surrendered, explains their brutality to Allied prisoners of war.

Very few Japanese soldiers took the option to surrender. A good example of this was the Battle of Saipan in 15 June-9 July 1944. Out of 32,000 Japanese soldiers, 24,000 were killed in action and another 5,000 committed suicide. With nowhere else to go, General Saito planned a final suicidal banzai charge which took place on 7 July 1944, saying, 'There is no longer any distinction between civilians and troops. It would be better for them to join in the attack with bamboo spears than be captured.' The 4,000 able bodied men who led the attack were followed by large numbers of walking wounded, even men on crutches, not even armed. The Americans knew about Japanese fanaticism, but they had never seen anything like this before.

Japan finally surrendered in August 1945, but some Japanese soldiers did not believe this was possible and stayed on islands in the Pacific ocean for years at the ready. The last of these men finally surrendered in around 1970.

The Imperial Japanese Army lost 2,121,000 men killed in the war. Figures for Japanese civilians who lost their lives vary greatly, ranging between 550,000 and 800,000.

CHAPTER FOUR

The Boshin War

The Boshin War was a Japanese civil war. It began on 27 January 1868 and ended with an Imperial victory, and the end of the Shogunate, on 27 June 1869.

At the commencement of the war, the Tokugawa Shogunate held power and were up against those intent on returning political control to the Japanese Imperial Court, which at the time was in the capital, Kyoto.

Many Japanese nobles and young samurai had become disillusioned with the Shogunate and their handling of the foreigner situation. Japan had opened its doors to the rest of the world in the mid-1850s and by now there were many Westerners in the country. The Shoguns seemed more interested in how much money they could make, rather than the cultural effect this was having.

Unfortunately for the Shogun, many of the samurai, particularly those from the western domains, the Choshu, Satsuma and Tosa, supported the Japanese Imperial Court. The Choshu samurai, descendants of the great Sengoku warlord Mori Motonari, had previously been supporters of the Tokugawa Shogunate.

The influence of the Choshu domain was evident in the appointment of Choshu Ito Hirobumi as the first Prime Minister of Japan, and the appointment of Omura Masujiro as the *hyobu daiyu,* the equivalent of Vice Minister of War, in the newly created Army-Navy Ministry. His job was to create a national army on the European model. He had previously done this in the Choshu domain; all he had to do now was replicate it on a grander scale. From his research and travel he knew that the best army was Napoleon's and the best Navy was that of Great Britain. At a meeting in June 1869 Omura said: 'If the government was determined to become militarily independent and powerful, it was necessary to abolish the fiefs and feudal armies, to do away with the privileges of the samurai class, and to introduce universal military conscription.'

Omura wanted the French Military Mission to be allowed to return to Japan and train his new army. He faced much opposition. One of his biggest critics were the samurai, who did not agree with his modernising reforms for the Japanese military. After all, if the authorities accepted Omura's recommendations, it could mean if not the end of the samurai, at least the end of their privileged position in society. The days of splendidly dressed men charging their enemy on horseback or on foot was over. The samurai sword, though razor sharp, was no match for the rifle bullet, let alone the machine gun.

On the evening of 9 October 1869, Omura, who had been in the Kansai region looking at sites for military schools, was out for a night with some friends in Kyoto drinking at a local inn when he was attacked by eight ex-samurai.

Omura was wounded several times but escaped by hiding in a bath full of dirty water. He made it to Osaka to be treated by a Dutch doctor, but on 7 December he died.

His assassins were soon arrested, tried, all found guilty and sentenced to death, but due to political pressure and because some government officials agreed with the defendants that Omura's reforms were an affront to the samurai class, they were reprieved. But with political change the following year, all eight were put to death.

Despite Omura's murder, his ideas for modernising Japan's military were implemented after his death. Since the beginning of the Meiji Restoration in 1871, the military had always had a strong influence in Japanese society and everyday life. During the Meiji period, nearly all of the nation's leaders were either samurai, ex-samurai or descendants of samurai, which meant that they would have all shared similar values. In 1873 the samurai lost its right to be the nation's only armed force, when a western-style conscripted army was brought into being.

Japan introduced military conscription under Field Marshal Yamagata Aritomo in 1873. It resulted in thousands of young Japanese men from all walks of life being taught patriotic military values, alongside an unwavering and unquestioning loyalty to the Emperor. Yamagata Aritomo had been watching with great interest the rapid improvements Prussia had been making in all aspects of their society. He was particularly taken with their notion of military expansion abroad while adopting an authoritarian government at home.

The well-educated, well-spoken and articulate Samurai didn't simply go away. Many opted to join the ranks of the new conscripted Imperial Japanese Army, most becoming officers. The new officer class became motivated, disciplined and highly trained.

Conscription and the dissolution of samurai status resulted in the samurai becoming *Shizoku*, which in English translates as 'warrior families'. The Shizoku had no special social privileges. They did keep their salaries, but lost the right to wear a Katana in public, as well as the right to execute commoners who showed them disrespect.

The government of Emperor Meiji brought in some radical changes aimed at reducing the power of the feudal domains, including the Satsuma domain. This resulted in the uprising led by Saigo Takamori.

The Satsuma domain was associated with the provinces of Satsuma, Osumi and Hyuga. It was men from this region who played a large part in the newly formed Meiji government and were prominent figures in it, certainly up to the outbreak of the First World War.

On 29 January 1877, the Satsuma Rebellion began. Certain members of the Satsuma Domain had become dissatisfied with the direction in which the country was heading, especially the samurai. Everything was changing around them, even their language and the clothes they wore were not the same any more. The *sonno-joi*, a Japanese and Chinese philosophy, declared 'expel the barbarian'. To many samurai, especially those who had fought on the side of the Imperial house to restore Imperial ways, this was a betrayal.

Saigo Takamori was a member of the Meiji government and had supported the new reforms, believing that he was part of a new, forward-thinking Japan. But he was concerned about growing political corruption. His slogan was *shinsei-kotoku*: 'new government, high morality'.

In the Seikanron debate of 1873, Saigo argued for Japan to go to war with Korea, because of her refusal to recognise the legitimacy of the Empire of Japan and its Emperor. Also Japanese envoys sent to Korea to establish trade and diplomatic relations had been badly treated. Saigo, himself a samurai, hoped for a role and glory for the thousands of Japanese samurai warriors who had found themselves out of work under Emperor Meiji's reforms. Saigo even offered to personally pay a visit to Korea to provoke a war. His plan was to visit Korea as a member of the Japanese government, to behave in such a manner that the Koreans would kill him, and in doing so allow Japan to declare war. His offer was rejected by the Japanese government. He resigned from the government in protest and returned home to Kagoshima in Kyushu. Many Satsuma who were also ex-samurai, members of the Japanese military and the Tokyo police service, also resigned and went home.

Saigo didn't give up. In 1874 he established a privately funded academy for ex-samurai, teaching Chinese classics as well as weapons training and the latest thinking in relation to military tactics. He also opened a school of artillery. The school had the support of the governor of Satsuma, who assisted further by appointing samurai graduates to local political positions, which allowed them to dominate the Kagoshima government.

It wasn't long before news of Saigo's military academies reached the ears of the authorities in Tokyo, and it was not well received. There had been several minor, yet extremely violent, samurai revolts in Kyushu, which government forces had managed to deal with, although it hadn't been easy. Saigo had made no direct threat against them, but he had such a devout following that the Japanese government was nervous.

In December 1876 an incident took place which nearly caused a war between Saigo's forces and the authorities in Tokyo. A man named Nakahara Hisao, along with 57 other men who were supposedly police officers which they may well have been, arrived in Kagoshima from Tokyo. They said they were there to investigate reports of subversive activities and general unrest. The men were captured by some of Saigo's followers, and when tortured they are reported to have admitted that they were government spies and had been sent to the area to assassinate Saigo.

Also in 1876 the samurai were banned from carrying swords. In place of the samurai the Meiji government had developed its own standing army and police force. They sent a warship to Kagoshima to remove weapons stockpiled at the arsenal, which in the main would have been samurai swords. Tensions were already running high because the government had removed samurai rice stipends. The warship arrived on 30 January 1877 and caused open conflict between Saigo's followers and the government soldiers. In Japanese history this is known as a sword hunt.

In response, a number of Saigo's academy students attacked the arsenal at Somuta and carried off a large quantity of swords.

Over the next few days, more than 1,000 students from Saigo's academy carried out further attacks on the naval yards and other arsenals. Saigo, although by now retired, was persuaded by his followers and students to come out and lead his men, a combination of experienced rebels and cadet students from his academy, against the central government in Tokyo.

The Meiji government did not want to escalate matters into full-scale war. They had to tread carefully. With this in mind they sent one of their warships, the *Takao*, under the command of Admiral Kawamura Sumiyoshi, along with Hayashi Tomoyuki, an official with the Home Ministry, to Kagoshima to ascertain a true picture of the situation. On their arrival the Governor of Satsuma, Oyama Tsunayoshi, explained to them that the reason for the uprising was that the government had sent men to their city to murder Saigo. The government had obviously put some thought in to this mission, as Admiral Kawamura was Saigo's cousin. Oyama asked Admiral Kawamura to come ashore in the hope that this would calm the situation. Then a number of rebel ships filled with armed men approached the *Takao* and attempted to board it. The attack was repelled by those on board. So Kawamura did not go ashore, saying that the current situation was too dangerous for him to leave the ship, and that the attempt to board the *Takao* constituted an offence against the Emperor Meiji and Imperial Japan.

With no progress being made, the *Takao* returned to Kobe, arriving on 12 February 1877. Hayashi Tomoyuki then met with General Yamagata Aritomo and Ito Hirobumi (later Prime Minister). It was decided that their best course of action was to send a section of the Imperial Japanese Army to Kagoshima to prevent the revolt from spreading.

Unknown to the authorities in Tokyo, on that same day Saigo was meeting with two of his most senior and experienced officers, General Kirino Toshiaki and General Shinohara Kunimoto. Saigo informed them that he intended marching on Kobe to ask questions of the government. Preparations were quickly made and they were soon ready to leave.

None of Saigo's troops were left at Kagoshima to protect his stronghold while he was away. He even rejected offers of support from surrounding domains. To give credence to his journey, Saigo set off for Kobe wearing his Japanese army uniform.

He and his men set off heading north, but were quickly hampered by some of the worst weather the region had witnessed in fifty years, with the deepest snowfall Satsuma had ever seen. Two days later Saigo and his men crossed into the Kumamoto region and approached the historic Kumamoto Castle, which was under the jurisdiction of its commandant General Tani Tateki, who had 3,800 soldiers and 600 policemen under his command. It was also the primary garrison town for the Imperial Japanese Army in the Kyushu region.

Saigo's arrival posed Tani something of a problem, because many of his officers were from Kagoshima and Tani feared that by opening his gates he ran the risk of desertions to Saigo's forces. So he stood firm.

On 19 February, some of the castle's defenders fired upon Saigo's men who were attempting to force their way in. Three hundred years old, it was one of the most formidable in Japan. Saigo was confident that if he could get in, the castle's peasant conscripts would be no match for his more experienced troops.

What Saigo didn't know was that inside the castle were a number of men who would eventually rise to positions of great rank within the Imperial Japanese army. They included Kabayama Sukenori who would become both a general and an admiral; Viscount Kodama Gentaro, a minister of the Meiji government who became a general instrumental in establishing the modern Imperial Japanese army; Viscount Kawakamo Soroku, a general in the Imperial Japanese Army and a chief military strategist in the First Sino-Japanese War; Count Nogi Maresuke, a general who became Governor General of Taiwan, a commander during the capture of Port Arthur from China in 1894, and a prominent figure during the Russo-Japanese war of 1904; and Count Oku Yasukata, who went on to become a field marshal.

On 22 February the main section of Saigo's army arrived at Kumamoto to join the attack. They engaged in a pincer movement on the castle. For Saigo and the Satsuma armies it was a good day, but still they failed to take the castle. As Saigo was losing a lot of men, he began to realise that he had underestimated his opposition. So he decided he would have to try to starve the castle's occupants into surrender. Not long before, the defenders had lost much of their food and ammunition in a warehouse fire, but Saigo didn't know that.

The siege continued for several weeks. During this time Saigo had his ranks swelled somewhat when a large number of ex-samurai from the surrounding Kumamoto countryside arrived to serve under his banner. But the stand-off between the two sides caused numerous problems for Saigo. The weather was cold and the ground rock hard and the longer the siege continued, the weaker his position became. Also he had to split his forces to enable him to hold a long defensive line from Tabaruzako to the Bay of Ariake, to ensure they were not surprised by the arrival of Imperial reinforcements sent to help relieve the castle.

Saigo was already in some difficulties as Imperial troops under General Yamagata had landed and taken his stronghold of Kagoshima, which meant no more supplies or reinforcements. An Imperial force of three warships, carrying 500 policemen and several companies of infantry, landed in Kagoshima on 8 March, seized the arsenals and captured the Satsuma governor.

Yamagata also landed a detachment of two infantry brigades and 1,200 policemen behind rebel lines so as to be able to advance on Kagoshima from Yatsushiro Bay. The Imperial forces landed with little in the way of opposition, marched north and seized the city of Miyanohara on 19 March. After waiting for reinforcements, Yamagata's forces, by then totalling 4,000 men, attacked the rear units of the Satsuma army and drove them back.

To make matters worse, on the evening of 8 April 1877, Saigo's lines that surrounded Kumamoto castle were breached by a number of Imperial soldiers from the castle. This resulted in supplies reaching the beleaguered men in the garrison, and four days later it was all over. A large force from the Imperial Army under Generals Kuroda Kiyotaka and Yamakawa Hiroshi arrived in Kumamoto forcing the heavily outnumbered Satsuma forces to retreat.

The defeat at Kumamoto was a massive setback for Saigo, which both demoralised and weakened his men. Although there were several more battles before the final one at Shiroyama, the defeat at Kumamoto castle was really the beginning of the end. The following battles became harder and harder as Saigo's numbers and supplies dwindled while they fought against ever-increasing Imperial forces.

Saigo spent the days immediately after his defeat at Kumamoto castle marching with the remainder of his army to Hitoyoshi. There they dug in and waited for the next onslaught by Imperial forces, uncertain how many more they could sustain. The government forces had also suffered, not as much as Saigo's, but the fighting was suspended for several weeks to allow both sides to recuperate and organise reinforcements. When they had replenished their forces, Saigo retreated to the city of Miyazaki, leaving behind groups of samurai fighters to conduct guerrilla attacks on the advancing Imperial forces.

Meanwhile, the Battle of Tabaruzaka began on 3 March 1877 and lasted for seventeen days, ending on 20 March. It was always going to be a one-sided affair, as the forces under General Yamagata numbered 90,000 men, while trying to fend them off were just 15,000 of Saigo's samurai. The samurai were eventually reduced to fighting with swords, as their supplies became depleted and their muzzle-loading rifles became sodden in the heavy rain. Each side lost about 4,000 men killed or wounded. Yamagata launched a full-on frontal assault on the rebel forces on 15 March, and by 20 March the samurai were forced to retreat, and although they tried to regroup in the town of Ueki, they were driven out.

Realising the precarious position he and his men were in, Saigo wrote a letter to Prince Arisugawa explaining why he was making his way to Tokyo and pointing out that he was not hell-bent on rebellion but just wanted a peaceful settlement. The Imperial Japanese government refused to negotiate, knowing full well that they would be able to sustain their position much longer than Saigo could.

The leaders of the government and the Imperial Japanese Army could sense victory was within their grasp. On 24 July 1877 they drove Saigo and his forces out of Miyakonjo, quickly followed by Nobeoka. They had already landed troops ahead of them at Oita and Saiki, just north of Saigo and his army. But despite their near encirclement they managed to escape. By now they had lost all of their artillery pieces and modern weapons, and their numbers had dwindled to just 3,000.

Saigo and his men decided to make a stand on the slopes of Mount Enodake. They were quickly surrounded. Yamagata was determined not to let them escape yet again, and sent in a force that outnumbered their enemy by seven to one. Many of Saigo's men committed suicide in the traditional manner, others surrendered.

Amazingly, Saigo and his remaining 500 men managed to escape, much to Yamagata's annoyance. Realising the end was near, the remainder of the Satsuma army made their way back to their home at Kagoshima, chased by Yamagata's men for seven days.

They arrived in Kagoshima on 1 September and immediately took to the slopes of Mount Shiroyama, which is 170 metres high and overlooks the city below, providing them with a formidable advantage over any enemy.

By the time soldiers of the Imperial Japanese army under General Yamagata and marines under Admiral Kawamuna Sumiyoshi arrived at Mount Shiroyama, they outnumbered what was left of Saigo's army sixty to one.

Yamagata had learned his lesson at Mount Enodake; he wasn't going to make the same mistake again. Over several days he had his men dig ditches, walls and obstacles around the base of the hill. Then he began a bombardment from five Imperial Navy vessels in Kagoshima harbour.

On 1 September 1877 Yamagata had a message delivered to Saigo asking that he and his men surrender. In the early hours of 24 September, no response having been received by Saigo, Yamagata ordered his men to carry out a frontal assault. By 6 am, only forty rebels remained alive. Saigo Takamori was dead. Shortly afterwards, the remaining rebels drew their swords and charged down Mount Shiroyama into the guns of the waiting Imperial forces. The Battle of Shiroyama marked the end of the Satsuma Rebellion.

The government's victory came at a price. They had spent so much money defeating Saigo and his men that Japan was forced off the gold standard and to print paper money. Most nations abandoned the gold standard as the basis of their monetary systems at some point in the twentieth century.

The rebellion had also marked the end of the samurai class, who had in effect been replaced by the new Imperial Japanese army, manned by conscripts from all classes.

After the memories of those turbulent days had faded somewhat, Saigo Takamori was seen by the people as a tragic hero. Probably with this in mind, and having no desire to antagonise the people, Emperor Meiji awarded him a posthumous pardon.

CHAPTER FIVE

Emperor Yoshihito

The Japanese Empire was a comparatively short-lived one. It had only three Emperors. Yoshihito was its second.

Born on 31 August 1879 at the Togu Palace in Tokyo, he was the son of the Emperor Meiji and would go on to become the 123rd Emperor of Japan.

The Emperor Meiji was married to the Empress Shoken, but Prince Yoshihito's mother was Yanagihara Naruko, one of his father's concubines – a lady in waiting of the Imperial House of Japan. She was the last concubine to provide a son for a reigning Japanese Emperor, as well as the last to give birth to a future Emperor of Japan.

Despite this, it was the Empress Shoken who was officially recognised as his mother. Both of Prince Yoshihito's elder siblings died when they were very young. He contracted meningitis within a few weeks of his birth, and although he recovered, his formative years were blighted by ill health.

As tradition dictated, as a child Prince Yoshihito didn't live with the Emperor and Empress at the Palace. Instead, until the age of 7 he lived with, and under the direct guidance of his great-grandfather, the Marquess Nakayama Tadayasu.

At 7 he moved to the Aoyama Detached Palace where he spent his mornings being educated in reading, writing and mathematics, as well as moral values. In the afternoon, after lunch, the Prince's learning became physical as he was taught how to play sports. This was more difficult for him because of his poor health.

When he was 8, rather than being taught on his own, he became part of a group of up to twenty privileged youngsters whose fathers were either members of the Japanese Imperial Family or Peers of the Empire of Japan. This school was called the *Gogakumonsho* and was within the grounds of Aoyama Detached Palace.

On the prince's eighth birthday his father announced he was to become his heir in waiting.

His education continued at the *Gakushuin* university, which is still in Tokyo today. But because of his health problems, he spent much of his time at the Imperial villas of Hayama and Numazu on the south coast, in the belief that the fresh sea air would be good for him.

Yoshihito excelled at languages, in particular French and Chinese, both of which he studied with the help of private tutors in the sumptuous surroundings of the Imperial Akasaka Palace.

When the Crown Prince was 20, the Emperor Meiji decided that it was time for his son to learn more about internal and international politics as well as more about the country's military matters. To begin with, he attended the House of Peers, the upper house of the Imperial Diet. He learned quickly and within a year hosted his first official reception for foreign diplomats in Tokyo. Over time, his exposure to western diplomats and their culture left him somewhat infatuated with their way of life. This did not go unnoticed, especially by the Emperor Meiji, and it wasn't always to his liking.

Still aged 20, the Crown Prince married the 15-year-old Kujo Sadako, who would later become the Empress Teimei. She was the daughter of Prince Kujo Michitaka, the leader of the Fujiwara Clan, a powerful family from the Yamato province.

Around the turn of the century, the Crown Prince spent much time touring Japan to acquire a greater understanding of the nation's people, their customs and how they lived.

Politically at the time, tensions were simmering in Europe, and between Russia and Japan. The Crown Prince was given the rank of Captain in the Navy, and Lieutenant Colonel in the Army. His duties, however, were entirely ceremonial, which usually meant visiting and inspecting military facilities and their personnel.

His reign as Emperor began on 30 July 1912, a month shy of his 33rd birthday, on the death of his father. Now more would be expected of him. He would be more in the public eye and his ailments, which were mostly of a neurological nature, would sooner or later be picked up on, and the position of Emperor being that of a figurehead, image was everything to Japan as a nation.

His condition worsened and his day-to-day interest in politics diminished. As the First World War got underway, it was his advisors, the Lord Keeper of the Privy Seal, and the ministers of the Imperial Household, who essentially determined the direction the country was taking. It wasn't difficult for these individuals to influence the Emperor's decisions.

As the First World War came to an end his condition worsened to such a degree that he was no longer able to attend the numerous official functions, or the annual manoeuvres conducted by the army or navy. Nor did he attend graduation ceremonies at the military academies, which the Emperor had traditionally always done. He was absent at the official opening of the Diet of Japan, neither did he perform the annual Shinto ritual ceremonies. Shinto played an extremely important part in Japanese life, so the Emperor's absence was a serious matter.

It was a situation that could not be allowed to continue, and on 25 November 1921 Crown Prince Hirohito was officially named Prince Regent.

The Great Kanto earthquake struck Japan just west of Tokyo on 1 September 1923. Measuring 7.9 on the Richter scale, it devastated large areas of the Kanto region including Tokyo and Yokohama and killed around 105,000 people. The earthquake caused a tsunami in Sagami Bay and its surrounding area, destroying some 570,000 homes and leaving two million people homeless.

The Emperor and the Empress had moved to Nikko, 140 kilometres north-east of Tokyo, a week before the earthquake and so survived. They were kept informed of the situation by carrier pigeon.

In December 1926, it was announced that the Emperor had pneumonia. He died on Christmas Day at the Imperial villa at Hayama in Sagami Bay. A four-mile-long procession accompanied his coffin as it was carried on an ox-drawn cart to its final resting place. As his funeral took place at night, the route was lit by small wood fires contained in iron lanterns.

CHAPTER SIX

Japan in the
First World War

In the First World War, the Japanese sided with the Allies. If Germany were defeated, Japan stood to gain Germany's territorial possessions in the Pacific region. Japan and the UK had been allies since the signing of the Anglo-Japanese Alliance on 30 January 1902 in London by Lord Landsdowne, the Secretary of State for Foreign Affairs, and Hayashi Tadasu, the Japanese diplomat mentioned previously.

Japanese Prime Minister Okuma Shigenobu and Foreign Minister Kato Takaaki wanted to seize the opportunity which the First World War provided Japan by increasing her influence in China. Japan intimated that she would be prepared to enter the war on the side of Britain and her allies if she was allowed to take over Germany's territories in the Pacific, and just days after the first shots were fired, on 7 August 1914, the British authorities contacted Tokyo asking them for their assistance by securing the Pacific sea lanes and stopping ships of the German Navy from carrying out attacks in Chinese waters. The Japanese were only too happy to acquiesce, and on 15 August 1914 demanded that Germany withdraw her warships from Chinese and Japanese waters and transfer Germany's Chinese concession of the port at Tsingtao/Qingdao to them. On 23 August Japan declared war on Germany and four days later began a blockade of Tsingtao.

On the same day, Japan sent a message to Vienna requesting that the Austro-Hungarian cruiser SMS *Kaiserin Elisabeth* be removed from Tsingtao. When this request was refused, Japan also declared war on Austria-Hungary.

On 2 September, soldiers of the Imperial Japanese Army invaded the Shandong province in China. Their target was the German settlement at Tsingtao.

Between October and December 1914, the Japanese Red Cross Society sent three medical teams to Europe, each consisting of a surgeon and twenty nurses. Two of the teams made their way to Paris, the third was sent to Southampton. The initial five-month deployment was increased to fifteen.

Naval operations against the Germans at Tsingtao began on 17 October 1914 and ended on 7 November with the surrender of German colonial forces. The siege of the port began on 31 October. Ships of the Imperial Japanese Navy under Vice-Admiral Sadakichi Kato arrived with dreadnoughts *Kawachi* and *Settsu*, battlecruisers *Konga* and *Hiei*, and the sea-plane carrier *Wakamiya* whose aircraft attacked targets on land and sea.

Two ships from the British Royal Navy, HMS *Triumph* and HMS *Usk*, assisted the Japanese in their blockade. According to German newspaper reports the *Triumph* was damaged by shore batteries, although this was not confirmed by the British authorities.

In October 1914 the Japanese navy invaded and captured several of Germany's Micronesian territories, including the Marianas, and the Caroline and Marshall Islands; all were taken with virtually no resistance. This was a decision taken by senior officers of the Imperial Japanese Navy without any discussion or agreement with members of the Japanese government.

In February 1915 there was a mutiny in Singapore by Indian troops of the 5th Light Infantry against the British government. Japanese marines who were on board their vessels at Singapore helped suppress the mutiny. The 5th Light Infantry had suffered poor leadership from its British officers. The Sepoys had been split into two groups, which was unpopular, and since being stationed in Singapore their diet had been changed. On 27 January 1915 their commanding officer, Colonel Martin, informed them that they were being transferred to Hong Kong. Some of the Sepoys got it into their heads that they were instead going to be sent to Europe or Turkey to fight against other Muslims.

The day before they were due to leave for Hong Kong, a farewell parade was held to see them on their way. Their commanding officer commented on the high standard of their turnout. After the parade the men needed to finalise the packing of the regiment's equipment and their own personal kit in preparation for boarding the SS *Nile* to sail to Hong Kong. On the afternoon of the parade, four companies out of the eight which made up the 5th Light Infantry mutinied. The Sepoys in the other four companies did not join in the mutiny but ran off in the confusion. Initially there was uncertainty amongst the British about what was going on. Two British officers were killed before they had time to recognise the seriousness of the situation.

The mutineers split up into three groups. One, which contained about 100 men, made its way to Tanglin Barracks, which was also where the bulk of the army's munitions were stored. Also at the barracks were 300 Germans who were been held there. The guards at the barracks were taken by surprise, the Sepoys opening fire without any warning. Ten British Guards were killed, three members of the Royal Johor Military Force, and a German internee.

Once inside the barracks the Sepoys tried to encourage the Germans to join them, even offering them rifles. They declined both the rifles and the request to join the mutiny, but thirty-five did take the opportunity to escape.

It was the Chinese New Year, which meant that most of the Chinese Volunteer Corps were on leave, meaning that large parts of the island were left unprotected.

Another of the groups made its way to Keppel Harbour and Pasir Panjang in the Queenstown area. On their way, they attacked anybody who remotely looked European. This took the lives of a further eighteen people.

The British declared martial law and sailors from HMS *Cadmus* went ashore to help.

On 16 February they requested the help of the Japanese. The vessels *Otowa* and *Tsushima* were sent immediately to Singapore. Although the help was sent, and well received by the Royal Navy in Singapore, the Japanese Navy was hesitant. The Commanding Officer of the Third Squadron, Rear Admiral Tsuchiya Mitsukane, had apparently expressed his displeasure in dispatching help as he believed that being a signatory of the Anglo-Japanese Alliance, Japan should not interfere in the internal affairs of another country without attaching conditions. To support his opinion, Tsuchiya recalled how previously a British ship that was anchored at Chilung refused to help the Japanese put down a Taiwanese revolt in Japan. Seeing that he had no choice but to follow orders from the Japanese government and naval headquarters, Tsuchiya secretly advised his land force not to kill or wound any Sepoy intentionally but to simply encourage them to surrender.

After the mutiny ended, more than 250 Sepoys were put on trial by court-martial. Of these, 47 were publicly executed by firing squad at Outram Road Prison. A further 73 were sentenced to periods of imprisonment ranging from 7 to 20 years.

The *Straits Times* included the following article the day after the executions: *An enormous crowd, reliably estimated at more than 15,000 people, was packed on the slopes of Sepoy Lines looking down on the scene. The square as before was composed of regulars, local volunteers and Shropshire under the command of Colonel Derrick of the Singapore Volunteer Corps (SVC). The firing party consisted of men from the various companies of SVC under Captain Tongue and Lieutenant Blair and Hay.*

The remaining Sepoys of the 5th, just under 600 men, and a few British and Indian officers, left Singapore on 3 July 1915 for the Cameroons and German East Africa. Their commanding officer, Colonel Martin, did not accompany them. He had been criticized by a court of inquiry and retired from the army soon after.

The court of inquiry, despite its 415 pages, was unable to conclusively determine the cause of the mutiny. It did however mention discord between the officers and men of the 5th Light Infantry, and the possibility that there may have been some German influences.

It was said at the inquiry that *'the prime cause of this lamentable episode was the responsibility of Colonel Martin… a loner for whom other officers had little respect. Martin's primary fault was that he was too trusting, to the point of naivety. While he cared for the welfare of his men and saw that their living conditions were improved, he was described as being too much of a "soldier's friend".'* Colonel Egerton of the India Office described the regiment's situation as 'a flock of sheep without a shepherd'.

As the war progressed, and realising that her European Allies were somewhat distracted by its events, Japan saw an opportunity to further strengthen her position in China. She did this by presenting the Chinese President Yuan Shikal with the 'Twenty-One Demands' on 18 January 1915. The demands came with the threat of dire consequences if they were rejected. There were five groups of demands:

> **Group 1** confirmed Japan's seizure of German ports and operations in the Shandong Province, and expanded Japan's sphere of influence over the province's railways, coasts and major cities.
>
> **Group 2** extended Japan's leasehold over the South Manchuria Railway Zone for 99 years and expanded her sphere of influence in southern Manchuria. It also demanded access to Inner Mongolia so Japan could exploit its raw materials, use it as a

manufacturing site, and use it as a strategic buffer against Russian encroachment in Korea.

Group 3 gave Japan control of the Han-Ye-Ping mining and metallurgical complex in central China, which was heavily in debt to Japan.

Group 4 prevented China from allowing any further coastal or island concessions to foreign powers.

Group 5 required China to hire advisors from Japan who could then effectively take control of China's finance and police. Japan would be allowed to build three major railway lines, as well as a number of Buddhist temples and schools. Japan would also gain effective control of Fujian.

The Chinese government attempted to stall as long as possible and leaked the contents of the Twenty-One Demands to European powers in the hope that they would perceive a threat to their own areas of interest and intervene. If China accepted the demands she would in essence become a Japanese protectorate and the revenues she received from European countries for the lease of territories would have become Japan's.

With growing international condemnation of her conduct, Japan finally agreed to change her demands on 26 April. The Group 5 demands were dropped and they resubmitted a reduced set of demands on 7 May. But this time the Chinese were given just two days to reply.

China was not in a position to go to war with Japan so her leaders had to accept the demands, and reluctantly signed the agreement on 25 May, Japanese Foreign Minister Kato Takaaki announcing to the world that the agreement was the idea of the Chinese authorities.

Throughout 1915 and 1916, German tried her best to negotiate a separate peace deal with Japan, but ultimately these efforts failed.

Japan and Russia signed a treaty on 3 July 1916. Part of the agreement saw both countries make a pledge that neither would make a separate peace with Germany. They endorsed that further by agreeing that if another nation threatened China, and in doing so this effected either of their own interests in the country, their response would be a united one. Both countries had massive interests in China, which neither wanted to give up.

The British Admiralty requested naval assistance from Japan on 18 December 1916. Japan replied that in return they required Britain to back her territorial claims on German possessions in Shandong, China, and the South Pacific. They didn't have to wait long for their answer. On 1 February 1917 Germany announced a resumption of unlimited submarine warfare and the British government agreed to Japan's request.

The Royal Navy's First Special Squadron, which carried out escort duties, were based at Singapore until 1917. Four of her destroyers were then sent to Malta to become part of the Mediterranean Fleet.

On 7 February 1917 Rear-Admiral Kozo Sato became commander of the 2nd Special Task Fleet, which consisted of seventeen destroyers that were sent to Malta as part of Japan's assistance to the Allied war effort as set out under the terms of the Anglo-Japanese Alliance. Sato, who commanded the two squadrons of destroyers from his flagship *Akashi*, arrived in Malta on 13 April 1917 and immediately began patrolling the eastern Mediterranean from Alexandria to Marseilles to Taranto. This greatly assisted the British. Sato's squadron carried out a total of 348 escort sorties from Malta, escorting 788 ships containing 700,000 soldiers. For their part, the Japanese lost 72 sailors killed in action. They rescued 7,075 people from damaged and sinking ships. This included the rescue of nearly 3,000 from the troopship SS *Transylvania* which was hit by a German torpedo on 4 May 1917. The Japanese did not lose a single ship during the deployment, but on 11 June 1917 the *Sakaki* was struck by a torpedo fired from the Austro-Hungarian submarine U-27 off Crete. Although it was not sunk, fifty-nine Japanese sailors were killed.

The USA entered the First World War with the Allies on 6 April 1917, meaning that she was on the same side as the Japanese, which was not an easy relationship for either nation as they had something of an acrimonious relationship as a result of their disagreements over China, as well as their attempts at domination of the Pacific region. To try to rectify this situation, both countries were signatories to the Lansing-Ishi Agreement that was signed on 2 November 1917 to help reduce tensions.

The Lansing-Ishi Agreement was in essence a diplomatic note. In the published text of the agreement, signed by Robert Lansing the US Secretary of State, and Ishil Kikujiro the Japanese special envoy, both parties agreed to uphold the 'Open Door Policy in China, with respect to its territorial and administrative integrity. The United States government also acknowledged that Japan had what they termed 'special interests' in China due to its geographic proximity to China, especially in those areas adjacent to Japanese territory – despite this being a contradiction of the Open Door Policy.

What wasn't made public was the agreement by both parties not to take advantage of opportunities that might arise in China as a result of the war, at the expense of Allied nations.

The British under Admiral Ballard gave praise to the Japanese and their quick response to all British requests for assistance. But the Japanese gained much from their involvement in assisting the Royal Navy: in particular they learnt all about British anti-submarine techniques, as well as gaining invaluable operational wartime experience. It also gave them the advantage of knowing what to expect should they ever have to engage the Royal Navy in a time of war. At the end of the war, the Imperial Japanese Navy returned home with seven German submarines as prizes, which greatly contributed to future Japanese submarine design and development.

Japan sent troops to Siberia in 1918, to assist Admiral Alexander Kolchak, the leader of the White movement, in his fight against the Bolshevik Army. Initially the Imperial Japanese Army had intended to send 70,000 troops to the area, but the United States opposed this, so it was greatly scaled back.

Besides sending soldiers, Japan also made equipment for some of the Allied nations. The years of the First World War proved extremely profitable for the Japanese and was a massive boost for the nation's industries. In international finance, Japan had gone from being a debtor nation to one in credit. For the first time in years, foreign money was pouring in to the country, with exports having quadrupled between 1913 and 1918.

On the other hand, Japan experienced price inflation, and in August 1918 suffered 'rice riots'.

Under Prime Minister Terauchi Masatake, the Japanese government oversaw a number of loans to the warlord Duan Qirui. These loans were administered between January 1917 and September 1918 to help persuade him to show favour to Japanese interests in China, as well as to help his cause in becoming ruler of northern China by defeating his rivals in a civil war. In return Japan was given the German concession at Kiautschou Bay in Shandong, control of the railways in Shandong, and other rights in Manchuria. Details of these loans were eventually leaked to the Chinese public, which left Duan Qirui in a difficult and embarrassing situation. Some of the concessions that were granted as a result of these loans were remarkably similar to those rejected in the 5th clause of the Twenty-One Demands. The popular discontent which grew out of the loans made to Duan Qirui grew in to what became known as the 'May Fourth Movement', which was an anti-imperialist, cultural, and political movement. On 4 May 1919, Chinese students protested against what they saw as their government's weak reaction to the Treaty of Versailles, which had allowed Japan to keep hold of territories in Shandong province that had previously been surrendered by Germany after the Siege of Tsingtao in 1914.

The Paris Peace Conference at the end of the First World War involved input from the representatives of thirty-two nations. The major decisions which came out of it were the creation of the League of Nations, five peace treaties with the defeated enemy states, the imposition of financial reparations upon Germany, and the drawing of new national boundaries.

Although there were representatives from 32 nations present, it was those from the five major powers of Britain,

France, Italy, Japan and the United States who actually controlled the conference.

One of the decisions made by the conference was the transfer to Japan of Germany's rights in Shandong. Japan was also given a mandate in relation to Germany's more northern Pacific islands – the South Pacific Mandate.

The presence of Japanese delegates in the Hall of Mirrors at Versailles at the signing of the treaty on 28 June 1919 was a culmination of fifty years of the transformation of Japan into a modern nation on the world stage. Japan had proved herself with her contribution to the Allied war effort in response to Britain's request for assistance in the 'waterways' of the Mediterranean and East Asia. Saionji Kinmochi sat alongside the 'Big Four': Lloyd George, Woodrow Wilson, Georges Clemenceau and Vittorio Emanuele Orlando.

The Western powers rejected Japan's bid for a clause to be included in the treaty on the issue of racial equality.

Hara Takashi had become Prime Minister of Japan in September 1918 and was determined to adopt a pro-western foreign policy. He had watched from the sidelines those who led his country through the First World War, and noted that neither Okuma Shigenobu nor Terauchi Masatake had attempted to strengthen ties with the United States or Great Britain. Takashi particularly wanted to support the League of Nations, but in Japan opinion was somewhat split on the topic. So Takashi came up with a compromise. Japan would support the League of Nations if they included a racial equality clause in their covenant.

Correcting what they saw as an inequality that needed changing became the most urgent international issue of the Meiji government. The Paris peace conference provided the Japanese delegation with the opportunity to achieve just that. The first draft of their proposal was presented to the League of Nations Commission on 13 February 1919 as an amendment to Article 21. Its wording was as follows:

> *The equality of nations being a basic principle of the League of Nations, the High Contracting Parties agree to accord as soon as possible to all alien nationals of states, members of the League, equal and just treatment in every respect making no distinction, either in law or in fact, on account of their race or nationality.*

Speaking at the conference, the diplomat Makino Nobuaki told the audience of dignitaries that during the First World War men of different races had fought together on the side of the Allies: 'A common bond of sympathy and gratitude has been established to an extent never before experienced.'

In the Western-dominated world of the day, which still involved the colonial rule over peoples of non-white nations, the Japanese proposal took the Western nations totally by surprise.

Lord Robert Cecil, British Under Secretary of State for Foreign Affairs, replied that the Japanese proposal was a 'very controversial one' and suggested it should not be discussed at all. Cecil was awarded the Nobel Peace Prize in 1937.

Next it was the turn of the Greek Prime Minister, Eleftherios Venizelos, who said that a clause banning religious discrimination should be removed from the covenant, as that was also a very controversial matter. This caused more debate and in the end Cecil had all clauses that forbade either racial or religious discrimination removed from the text of the peace treaty.

By this time, the racial equality clause was beginning to draw widespread public attention, especially in Japan, where demonstrations demanded the end of what had become known as the 'badge of shame'. At the time, Japanese nationals were not allowed to emigrate to the United States, Canada, Australia or New Zealand. But in the United States the proposal received a negative press, especially in those parts of the country where slavery had been part of everyday life just a couple of generations earlier. The western states of the USA also feared mass Chinese and Japanese immigration.

The Chinese delegation, despite being at daggers drawn with the Japanese over the question of who was receive the former German colony of Qingdao together with the rest of the German concessions in Shandong province, said they would support the racial equality clause. But a member of the Chinese delegation declared that the Shandong question was far more important to his government at that time than the racial equality clause.

The Australian Prime Minister Billy Hughes, who was born in London to Welsh parents and had emigrated to Australia in 1884, announced that 'ninety-five out of one hundred Australians rejected the very idea of equality.' Hughes had entered politics as a trade unionist, and like most of the Australian working class was very strongly opposed to Asian immigration to Australia. He believed that accepting the racial equality clause would

Emperor Showa, 1928.

Japanese Rising Sun flag.

The Chōshū Kiheitai.

Japanese soldiers invading Andaman Islands.

Atomic Bomb, Nagasaki, 1945.

Funeral Emperor Meiji.

Dead Japanese soldiers at Tarawa, Second World War.

Above: A Japanese Tanto.

Right: Prince Asaka in military uniform.

Japanese soldiers in the Second World War.

Crown Prince Hirohito and Lloyd George, 1921.

Enthronement of Emperor Taisho on 30 July 1912.

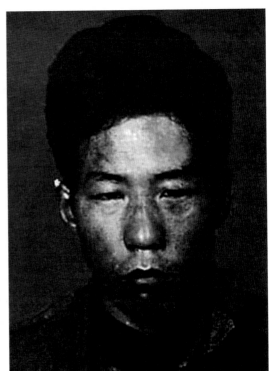

Above left: Hideki Tojo.

Above right: Daisuki Namba.

Kenji Doihara. War Crimes trial, Tokyo 1946.

Japanese surrender to America in 1945.

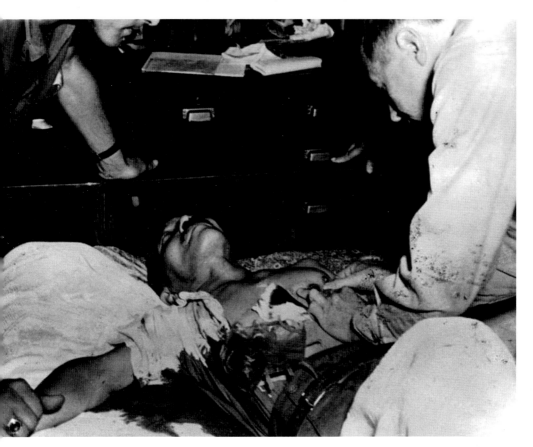

Suicide of Hideki Tojo, 1945.

Above left: Japanese prisoner of war being searched by British Soldier, 1945.

Above right: Kumamoto Castle, 1874.

Hirohito Shirayuki.

Above left: Emperor Meiji, 1873.

Above right: Emperor Meiji's mother, Nakayama Yoshiko, 1875.

Japanese prisoners of war, Tarawa, 1945.

Japanese soldiers in Singapore, Second World War.

Japanese attack on Pearl Harbour, 1941.

Battle of Saipan beach defences, 1944. (*GravityIsForSuckers, CC BY-SA 4.0*)

Boxer Rebellion, 1900.

Battle of Shanghai, 1932.

Siege of Peking, 1900.

Nanking massacre, 1937.

Kazuo Sakamaki. First Japanese prisoner of war, captured at Pearl Harbour, 1941.

Depiction of Emperor Meiji receiving the Order of the Garter, 1906.

Japanese soldiers on outskirts of Mukden, Manchuria, 1931.

Japanese Foreign Affairs Secretary, Mamoru Shigemitsu, signs the document of surrender aboard the USS *Missouri* in Tokyo Bay.

mean the end of the White Australia immigration policy that had been adopted in 1901. This was somewhat ironic considering that long before Australia had been colonised by white Europeans its inhabitants had been non-white. Hughes added: 'No government could live for a day in Australia if it tampered with a white Australia. The position is this, either the Japanese proposal means something or it means nothing. If it is the former, out with it; if the latter, why have it?' At the conference Hughes secured for Australia control of the former German possession of New Guinea.

The New Zealand Prime Minister William Massey was next to voice his disagreement with the Japanese proposal of the Racial Equality Clause, though not quite as vociferously as Hughes had done.

Having listened politely and intently to the comments and observations that had been made by a number of delegates, all of whom were against his proposal, Nobuaki told a press conference in Paris.

We are not too proud to fight but we are too proud to accept a place of admitted inferiority in dealing with one or more of the associated nations. We want nothing but simple justice.

France declared its support for Nobuaki's proposal; they had always believed French language and culture to be 'civilizing' forces open to all peoples. This was refreshing for the Japanese delegation to hear.

David Lloyd George, the British Prime Minister, found himself in a difficult position. He wanted to keep the nations of the British Empire, who were present at the conference, united, which in essence meant voting against the proposal. But Britain and Japan had signed an alliance in 1902, so Japan, understandably, would have expected Britain's support.

General Jan Smuts, the South African Prime Minister, and Sir Robert Borden, the Prime Minister of Canada, went to visit Nobuaki and Count Chinda Sutemi, the Japanese Ambassador to the UK. Their intention was to work out a compromise while the Australian Prime Minister, Hughes, acted as a mediator. The meeting did not end well. The Japanese delegation later described Hughes as a 'vulgar peasant' and 'loud and obnoxious'. In response, Hughes said the Japanese had 'beslobbered me with genuflections and obsequious deferences'. Despite this, Borden and Smuts somehow managed to persuade Hughes to accept the racial equality clause, provided it did not affect the issue of immigration.

Borden and Smuts took the compromise back to Nobuaki and Sutemi, but they turned it down.

The proposal also caused problems for the United States President, Woodrow Wilson, who was a supporter of racial segregation in his own country and in need of the votes of segregationist Southern Democrats if the Senate was to ratify the League of Nations treaty. Strong opposition to the proposal from the delegations of the British Empire gave him the excuse he needed to reject it.

The final session of the commission took place on 11 April 1919. Makino reiterated the Japanese position on the matter of human rights and racial equality. Robert Cecil confirmed the British Empire's opposition to it. Vittorio Orlando, the Italian Prime Minister, agreed with the statement on human rights but did not support the racial equality proposal. French Senator Léon Bourgeois was in support of the racial equality proposal as it embodied 'an indisputable principle of justice'.

The Commission's chairman was Woodrow Wilson, who determined that the vote had to be unanimous rather than a simple majority. Eleven out of the seventeen delegates voted in favour of the proposal, and so the amendment was defeated.

The Japanese delegation demanded that the transcript of the conference included the fact that a clear majority had voted for the amendment.

Wilson then promised to support the Japanese claims on the former German possessions and concessions held in China if they would accept the rejection of the racial equality proposal. In addition, and against the advice of his naval commanders, Wilson agreed to support Japan's claims to the Pacific islands of the Mariana, Marshall and Caroline islands, which she had occupied in 1914. However Japan would only be allowed to administer the islands under the mandate of the League of Nations and not annex them outright.

However, in the 1920s Japan began to ignore the conditions of the mandate, preventing representatives of the League of Nations from visiting the islands. She started to bring Japanese settlers to the islands and began militarising them, most noticeably Truk where she built the biggest Japanese naval base in the Pacific region.

The Paris Peace Conference had been comprehensively covered in the Japanese media, and public opinion was galvanised against the United States. Japan's westernizing ambitions took a step back, and henceforth she became more inward looking.

Wilson's decision to veto the Japanese proposal on racial equality in part led to race riots back home in America. The votes of the Southern Democrats were not enough to get the treaty ratified by the United States Senate, meaning that the Americans never actually joined the League of Nations.

Having read and researched the events of the Paris Peace Conference, I can't help but believe that the lack of support for Japan's racial equality proposal is connected to her actions which resulted in her ending up at war with Britain and her dominion nations and the United States. Prime Minister Hara Takashi initially wanted to adopt a pro-western approach on the international stage, but Wilson's decision effectively snubbed the Japanese by implying they were a race of second class people.

In 1923, the Anglo-Japanese Alliance, in place since 30 January 1902, expired and Japan started to build closer relationships with Germany and Italy.

CHAPTER SEVEN

America and Japan in the 1920s and 1930s

Through the 1920s, despite underlying tensions, America and Japan had a reasonably cordial trading relationship.

But Japan invaded Manchuria on 18 September 1931 and over the following years continued expanding into China.

On 1 July 1937 the Second Sino-Japanese War began. It didn't come to an end until Japan surrendered at the end of the Second World War. It is estimated that somewhere between 17 and 22 million Chinese civilians died as a result of the Japanese invasion and occupation. America did little to intervene until Japan attacked her Pacific Fleet at Pearl Harbor at the end of 1941.

The Nanking massacre of December 1937–January 1938 prompted the United States, the United Kingdom and France to help China by providing loans to purchase war supplies.

Then there was the unprovoked attack on the USS *Panay* on 12 December 1937 while it was moored outside Nanking on the Yangtze River. The *Panay* was part of the US Navy's Yangtze Patrol whose duty was to protect American lives and property in China. One of her officers, Lieutenant J.W. Geist, told how the day before the attack they had spoken with Japanese soldiers in the area informing them who they were and what they were doing and pointing out the three American flags clearly visible on the ship. After the initial attack, Japanese aircraft machine-gunned the small boats that were taking the wounded from the *Panay* to shore to receive medical attention.

A *Times* correspondent, Colin MacDonald, who had been aboard the *Panay*, recalled how he had seen a small Japanese army boat machine-gunning the *Panay* as it was sinking. The *Panay* had evacuated the remaining Americans from Nanking. Aboard were 5 naval officers, 54 enlisted men, 4 US Embassy staff, and 10 civilians, including cameraman Norman Alley of Universal Newsreel, Eric Mayell of Movietone News, the *New York Times*'s Norman Soong, Jim Marshall, the correspondent for *Colliers Weekly*, Sandro Sandri, the correspondent for *La Stampa*, and Luigi Barzini Junior, the correspondent of the *Corriere della Sera*.

On 12 December the Japanese air force was informed that ten large steamers and a number of junks had been sighted on the Yangtze River just upstream from Nanking with a number of fleeing Chinese forces on board. Anchored in that same location were the *Panay* and three Standard Oil tankers. Without any warning, the *Panay* was attacked by three bomber and nine fighter aircraft of the Imperial Japanese Navy. The Yokosuka B4Y Type-96 bombers dropped eighteen 132lb bombs, two of which struck the *Panay* while she was being strafed by the fighter aircraft.

The *Panay* sank, four aboard were killed, including Sandri of *La Stampa*, and forty-eight were wounded.

The three oil tankers were also attacked and destroyed. The captain of one of the tankers, the *Mei An*, was killed along with a number of Chinese civilians. The tankers had been helping to evacuate the families of Standard Oil's employees.

On 26 January 1938, at the time of the Nanking Massacre, John M. Allison, a consul at the American Embassy in Nanking, was struck in the face by a Japanese soldier for no apparent reason. The Japanese Consul General in the city, Katsuo Okatsuo, officially apologized for the incident, but only after the Americans had demanded that they do so. The Allison incident, along with the subsequent looting of American property in Nanking, put pressure on the already strained relations between Japan and the United States.

On 22 September 1940 Japanese forces invaded French Indochina (now Vietnam) in an attempt to stop supplies, mainly arms and oil, from reaching China. The supplies were imported through Indochina along the Kunming-Hai Phong railway, having arrived at the port of Haipong.

America responded by stopping shipments of aeroplane parts, tools and aviation fuel. Japan viewed this as an unfriendly act. America did not however cease her oil exports to Japan, in part because of feelings in Washington. Japan was almost entirely dependent on other countries for its oil, American was a vital supplier, and politically it was felt that such an act would be extremely provocative.

In the middle of 1940, President Franklin D. Roosevelt took the decision to move his Pacific Fleet from its established base at San Diego to its new home at Pearl Harbor in Hawaii. At the same time he also ordered a military build-up in the Philippines. Both decisions had been taken to discourage the Japanese from continuing their policy of aggression in the Far East.

For some reason which isn't abundantly clear, the Japanese High Command convinced themselves that if they attacked any of Britain's Southeast Asian colonies, such as Burma, Malaya, Hong Kong or Singapore, the United States would mobilise their Pacific Fleet and intervene to assist the British. They concluded that it was necessary to carry out a preventative strike at Pearl Harbor to put the American Pacific Fleet out of action.

There is actually no evidence to suggest that America would have entered the war to help Britain protect her Asian colonies. Although it would have been somewhat of a calculated risk, Japan could just have gone ahead and attacked Hong Kong, Burma, Malaya and Singapore, and America still may not have entered the war at that time.

In July 1941, the United States did stop exporting oil to Japan, after Japan's seizure of French Indochina after the fall of France to Nazi Germany. Without any oil coming from America, the Japanese proceeded with plans to take the oil rich Dutch East Indies, although this was the choice of the Imperial Japanese Navy and not the Army, who much preferred the idea of invading Russia to acquire oil.

Since July 1940 the American President had had the authority to control exports to foreign countries in the interest of American security, and had shown previously that he did not shrink from the tough decisions of cutting off shipments to Japan of scrap metal, aviation fuel and machine tools. To include oil among the exports to be restricted was a sterner message. By stopping oil exports to Japan, he had virtually compelled the Dutch and the British to join the United States in going up against Japan. These were delicate times. Unless the Dutch and the British were willing to dissociate themselves completely from America's Far Eastern policy, they had to take a similar stance. But it wasn't all one sided. By forcing this choice on the Dutch and British, the United States would were implicitly stating that if they followed the American lead in denying oil to Japan, the United States would have an obligation to defend their Far Eastern possessions. This in turn would mean that Japan would have to choose either to meet the American conditions for lifting the oil embargo – the evacuation of their military forces from the Asiatic mainland – or to secure, by seizing the Dutch East Indies, a ready-made supply of oil on their own terms, in the face of the strongly implied American commitment to oppose such action with military force.

If Japan were to invade the Dutch East Indies they had to do it sooner rather than later as they only had a few months' supply of oil left. Also, the longer they took, the more time America had to build up her military strength in the region.

Japan and the United States engaged in negotiations throughout 1941. The Japanese offered to withdraw their forces from most of China and Indochina after making peace with China's Nationalist government. They also proposed to adopt an independent interpretation of the Tripartite Pact that they had signed with Germany and Italy on 27 September 1940 in Berlin, and to refrain from trade discrimination, provided all other nations reciprocated. Somewhat surprisingly, Washington rejected these proposals. The Japanese Prime Minister Konoye then offered to meet with President Roosevelt, but Roosevelt insisted that the two countries reach an agreement before any meeting took place.

The United States ambassador to Japan repeatedly urged President Roosevelt to accept the offer of the meeting with the Japanese Prime Minister, warning that it was the only way to preserve the conciliatory Japanese government and peace in the Pacific, but Roosevelt would not do so. The Konoye government collapsed the following month when the Japanese military rejected a withdrawal of all of its troops from China.

Despite the change of government, Japan sent the Americans another proposal on 20 November. It included an offer to withdraw from southern Indochina and to refrain from any further attacks in Southeast Asia, but in return it wanted the United States, the United Kingdom, and Holland to cease providing aid to China and to lift their sanctions against Japan. Rather than accept the Japanese offer, the Americans came up with a counter-offer of their own. It was delivered by the American Ambassador in Tokyo on 27 November and has become referred to as the 'Hull Note' after Secretary of State Cordell Hull. This was the final proposal delivered to the Empire of Japan by the USA before Japan attacked the Pacific Fleet at Pearl Harbor and Japan's declaration of war. The Japanese considered it to be an ultimatum. The Hull Note required Japan to completely evacuate China without conditions and conclude non-aggression pacts with Pacific powers. Despite negotiations continuing, on 26 November, the day the note was delivered, the Japanese task force had left port and were on their way to attack Pearl Harbor.

Preliminary planning for an attack on Pearl Harbor had begun in early 1941 under the guidance of Admiral Isoroku Yamamoto, then the commander of Japan's Combined Fleet. He won approval for formal planning and training for the attack from the Navy General Staff after threatening to resign if he didn't get his way on the matter. Planning was underway by early spring 1941. Emperor Hirohito did not give the plan permission to go ahead until 1 December.

There were problems with the attack. As Pearl Harbor was in relatively shallow waters, any ships they sank would not fully sink below the waterline and all would be easily salvageable. And loss of manpower would be nowhere near what they would have liked, as many of the men would be on shore leave and many of the ships were running below recognised manning levels. Also, which the Japanese knew, the three aircraft carriers, *Enterprise, Lexington* and *Saratoga*, were not at Pearl Harbor. Despite this, Yamamoto, still decided to go ahead.

CHAPTER EIGHT

The Mukden Incident

The 1930s saw the Japanese Empire at its peak. With the Second World War still more a possibility than a certainty, it continued to flourish with its territories stretching from mainland China to Micronesia. But Japan was not satisfied with what she had achieved, she wanted more, and it was this greed that would be her eventual downfall.

In 1931, believing that a conflict in Manchuria would be in Japan's best interests, and acting in the spirit of the Japanese concept of *gekokujo,* or overthrowing or surpassing one's superiors, Kwantung Army Colonels Seishiro Itagaki and Kanji Ishiwara came up with a plan that would allow Japan to invade Manchuria by provoking an incident from Chinese forces stationed nearby. They chose as their target the rail section in an area near Liutiao Lake. The area had no official name and had no militarily importance, but it was only eight hundred metres away from the nearby Chinese garrison of Beidaying, where troops under the 'Young Marshal' Zhang Xueliang were stationed. The Japanese plan was simply to set off an explosion and then blame the Chinese for having caused it.

In the event, the explosion was so small and the damage to the railway was so minor that minutes later a train passed over it unharmed and reached its destination at Shenyang.

On the morning of 19 September 1931, two artillery pieces which had been installed at the Mukden officers' club opened fire on the nearby Chinese garrison in response to the alleged Chinese attack on the railway. Zhang Xueliang's small air force was destroyed and his soldiers fled from their destroyed barracks as five hundred Japanese troops attacked the Chinese garrison of around seven thousand men. The Chinese troops were no match for the more experienced Japanese soldiers. By the evening, the fighting was over and the Japanese had occupied Mukden at the cost of five hundred Chinese lives while losing only two of their own.

The Imperial Japanese Army accused Chinese dissidents of the act and responded with a full invasion of the country which led to the occupation of Manchuria, in which Japan established the puppet state of Manchukuo six months later.

The deception was exposed by the Lytton Report of 1932, leading Japan to diplomatic isolation, and in March 1933 it was forced to withdraw from the League of Nations.

In 1931 the League of Nations carried out an investigation into Japan's invasion and seizure of Manchuria by looking in to the Mukden Incident, under what became known as the Lytton Commission, which consisted of five members: Victor Bulwer-Lytton, the 2nd Earl of Lytton, who headed the Commission; United States Major General Frank Ross McCoy; Dr Heinrich Schnee, who had been the last Governor of German East Africa and later represented the Nazi Party in the Reichstag;

Luigi Aldrovandi Marescotti, Italian ambassador to Buenos Aires; and General Henri Claudel of France. The Japanese delegates walked out of the League of Nations when the League supported China on the matter.

The commission announced its findings in October 1932. It said that Japan had wrongfully invaded Manchuria and that she should hand it back to the Chinese. It also stated that the Japanese puppet state of Manchukuo should not be recognised internationally.

The following piece is taken from an article about the Mukden Incident of 1931:

> *According to Akira Fujiwara, Hirohito endorsed the policy of qualifying the invasion of China as an 'incident' instead of a 'war'; therefore he did not issue any notice to observe international law in this conflict (unlike what his predecessors did in previous conflicts officially recognized by Japan as wars), and the Deputy Minister of the Japanese Army instructed the Chief of staff of the Japanese China Garrison Army on August 5 not to use the term 'prisoners of war' for Chinese captives. This instruction led to the removal of the constraints of international law on the treatment of Chinese prisoners. The works of Yoshiaki Yoshimi and Seiya Matsuno show that the Emperor also authorized, by specific orders (rinsanmei), the use of chemical weapons against the Chinese. During the invasion of Wuhan, from August to October 1938, the Emperor authorized the use of toxic gas on 375 separate occasions, despite the resolution adopted by the League of Nations on May 14 condemning Japanese use of toxic gas.*

CHAPTER NINE

Emperor Hirohito

Emperor Hirohito was the spiritual leader of Japan although how much power he actually had is debateable. He was born on 29 April 1901 at the Togu Palace in Tokyo, the first son of Crown Prince Yoshihito who would later become the Emperor Taisho during the reign of his grandfather, Emperor Meiji. As a child he was known as Prince Michi. In keeping with the tradition of the day, seventy days after his birth he was sent to live with another family. Count Kawamura Sumiyoshi, a retired vice-admiral, brought him up as if he were his own child, as he also did with the Prince's brother, Prince Yasuhito.

But when Prince Michi was 3, Kawamura died and he and his brother Yasuhito returned to live at the Imperial Court, initially at the Imperial mansion in Numazu, Shizuoka, and after that at the Aoyama Palace.

He was 11 when his grandfather, the Emperor Meiji, died on 30 July 1912, making him heir apparent to his father Yoshihito, the new Emperor. Now known as Hirohito, it was decided that the prince should begin his military service. He was commissioned as a Second Lieutenant in the Imperial Japanese Army and as an ensign in the navy. In 1914 he was promoted to the rank of lieutenant in the army and sub-lieutenant in the navy, and two years later he was promoted to captain in the army and lieutenant in the navy. In the same year, 1916, he was formally proclaimed Crown Prince and heir apparent, and in 1920 he received further military promotions, becoming a major in the army and a lieutenant commander in the navy.

In 1921, to enhance the good relations Japan had built up with her European allies, Hirohito was sent on a six month tour of Europe, visiting Belgium, France, Holland, Italy, and the United Kingdom.

On his return to Japan, his father's health was on the decline and he was suffering bouts of mental illness, and on 29 November 1921 Hirohito was made the Regent of Japan. This was an interesting time politically, and one when he greatly needed the good council of his advisers.

He had only been Regent for two weeks when the Four Power Treaty on Insular Possessions was signed with Britain, France and the United States. The treaty was an agreement between the four nations to recognise the status quo in the Pacific region. Japan and Britain also agreed to formally terminate the Anglo-Japanese Alliance which had originally been signed on 30 January 1902.

The Washington Naval Agreement, also known as the Five Power Treaty, was signed in Washington on 6 February 1922 by France, Italy, Japan, the UK and the USA. Its purpose was to prevent an arms race by limiting each country's permitted naval construction.

Japan withdrew its troops from the Siberian Intervention on 28 August 1922. The Siberian Intervention had seen troops from the Entente Powers dispatched to assist White Russian forces against Soviet Russia and its allies during the Russian civil war.

On 27 December 1923, Daisuke Nanba, a Japanese student and communist agitator, tried to assassinate Prince Regent Hirohito. This is known as the Toranomon Incident. Hirohito was on his way to the opening of the 48th Imperial Diet in Tokyo in a horse-drawn carriage when Nanba approached as the carriage slowed at a junction. Holding a small pistol in his right hand, he aimed it at the Prince Regent's carriage and fired just one bullet. It missed Hirohito and hit one of his chamberlains, who injured but not badly.

Nanda was the son of a member of the Diet, but that didn't save him. His actions were motivated in part by his leftist ideology, as well as a desire to revenge for the death of Shusi Kotoku, a Japanese socialist and anarchist executed in 1910 as part of the High Treason Incident of 1910, an attempt to assassinate the Emperor Meiji. Nanba was found guilty, sentenced to death on 13 November 1924, and executed two days later.

Prince Hirohito married Princess Nagako, the future Empress Kojun, who was also his distant cousin, and the daughter of Prince Kuniyoshi Kuni, on 26 January 1924. The Prince was 22 years old and the Princess was 23. After their marriage the Emperor decided against retaining any of his thirty-nine court concubines.

Hirohito became the Emperor of the Empire of Japan on Christmas day 1926, after the death of his father, the Emperor Yoshihito, and remained in power until the end of the Empire in 1947. He then stayed on as the Emperor, but of the State of Japan, which replaced the old Empire. He held that position for 42 years until his death on

7 January 1989 when he was succeeded by his eldest son, Akihito, who after thirty years as Emperor abdicated on 30 April 2019.

When Hirohito came to power in 1926, Japan was already one of the world's major powers. It was one of the four permanent members of the League of Nations, it had the third largest navy, and it had the ninth largest economy in the world. But this didn't mean that everything ran smoothly for Hirohito. In the early part of his reign Japan was hit by a financial crisis and, having been in credit since the Great War, became a debtor nation again.

In 1927 Japan experienced the 'Showa Recession' which, added to political instabilities, contributed to the rise of Japanese militarism, which set the nation on its path to the Second World War, and ultimately the end of the Empire.

The Showa Financial Crisis took place during the first year of Hirohito's reign. It brought down the government of Japanese Prime Minister Wakatsuki Reijiro, which led to the Japanese banking industry being dominated by industrial and financial conglomerates until the end of the Second World War.

The Showa financial crisis wasn't the only problem Hirohito had to worry about. He had to watch while the different branches of the military gained more power within the government. Already since 1900 the Imperial Japanese Army and Navy had held the power of veto over government cabinets.

On 9 January 1932, in what was known as the Sakuradamon Incident, Lee Bong-chang, a Korean independence activist, tried to assassinate the Emperor Hirohito by throwing two hand grenades at him outside the Sakuradamon gate of Tokyo's Imperial Palace. Hirohito escaped unscathed, although one of his guards was injured. Lee had moved to Japan when he was 25, been adopted by a Japanese family in Osaka, and took the Japanese name of Kinoshita Shoichi. In 1931 he joined the Korea Patriotic Legion and became involved in the plot to assassinate the Emperor Hirohito. Lee was arrested at the scene, tried in secret, sentenced to death, and hung at Ichigaya Prison, Tokyo, on 10 October 1932.

Moving forward to the Second World War, it is important to remember that under Hirohito's leadership, Japan was a partner of the Tripartite Pact with Germany and Italy, which formed the Axis Powers, although, other than being at war with China, she was not actually involved in the Second World War. But by being part of the Axis Powers, it became clear on whose side she would be if and when she entered the war at any time.

Any doubts Hirohito might have had about being involved with the Axis Powers dissolved when he saw the successes being achieved by the Wehrmacht and Nazi Germany in Europe.

As time went on it became clear that it was more a matter of when than if Japan would be going to war. A Japanese Government Cabinet meeting took place on 4 September 1941 to discuss war plans prepared by the Imperial General Headquarters. Out of that meeting came the following decision:

> *Our Empire, for the purpose of self-defence and self-preservation, will complete preparations for war and is resolved to go to war with the United States, Great Britain, and the French if*

necessary. Our Empire will concurrently take all possible diplomatic measures vis-à-vis the United States and Great Britain, and thereby endeavour to obtain our objectives. In the event that there is no prospect of our demands being met by the first ten days of October through the diplomatic negotiations mentioned above, we will immediately decide to commence hostilities against the United States, Britain and the French.

From that communiqué, it is clear that the Japanese were determined to go to war, and if the time had been right for them to do so they would have done so well before the attack on Pearl Harbor three months later. However, it appears to have been more the chiefs of the Army and Navy General Staffs who wanted war than Hirohito himself, as the Emperor had always previously courted diplomatic negotiations, and only planned for war if negotiations failed.

Hirohito was Emperor when General Hideki Tojo became Prime Minister of Japan on 17 October 1941, a position which held until being forced to resign on 22 July 1944. Tojo was a staunch army man, but had spoken out against war with the United States before the attack on Pearl Harbor.

But the invasions by Japan and occupations of countries and islands throughout Asia and the Pacific took place while Hirohito was Emperor and Tojo was Prime Minister, as did the many war crimes that were carried out by Japanese forces against both civilians and Allied prisoners of war.

It was almost as if Hirohito wanted Tojo as Prime Minister to forge better relations with the Army, and to supress and control the extreme opinions which prevailed amongst some of the upper echelons of the Imperial Japanese Army.

The Prime Minister before Tojo was Fumimaroe Konoe. Konoe favoured Prince Naruhiko Higashikuni to be the next Prime Minister. Hirohito however did not agree with Konoe. He was against a member of the Japanese Royal Family holding the post, as eventually he might have to carry the responsibility for defeat in a war against the Allied nations, which could ruin the prestige of the House of Yamato. Instead the Emperor chose Tojo, who was known for his devotion to the Imperial Empire.

It is interesting to note that Tojo was arrested at the end of the war, put on trial, found guilty of war crimes and sentenced to death. Would the same have happened to Prince Naruhiko if he had been Prime Minister instead of Tojo? I doubt it. After all, Hirohito walked away scot free.

After the battles of Midway and Leyte, it became clear to Emperor Hirohito that the situation for Japan was dire. But despite this, all of his advisors were telling him to continue with the war. Only one voice stood up and said No, that of ex-Prime Minister Konoe. He urged a negotiated surrender, fearing that Japan could fall victim to a communist revolution, a fear he held greater than that of defeat in the war. But the Emperor did not agree.

Emperor Hirohito believed that if his forces could achieve just one more decisive victory, he would be better placed in any subsequent surrender negotiations with the Allies, so he dismissed Konoe's sound advice. Matters didn't improve for Japan, they became worse. In April 1945 Japan received news from Russian that she would not be renewing her neutrality agreement with her, and in May her ally Germany surrendered unconditionally to the Allies across Europe, making it clear that Japan was now going to be up against the entire forces of the Allied nations, who would no longer have to divide their forces.

The Japanese government held a cabinet meeting in June 1945. Even though it must have been obvious to everybody at that meeting that the war was lost and it was simply a matter of time before their Empire came crashing down around them, remarkably the decision was to continue the fight to the last man. The decision was ratified at an Imperial Council meeting soon afterwards, and although Emperor Hirohito was present, he did not speak.

These were strange times for Japan and her Emperor. Decisions had now become less about military victories and losses, and more about whether common sense should have more meaning than personal and national shame and dishonour. Despite some well-placed government individuals having fully grasped the hopeless military situation the country was in, and that a negotiated settlement was the only sensible way to go, more extreme elements were calling for 'a death before dishonour mass suicide'. It had now become a battle of common-sense over madness.

On 26 July 1945, the Allied High Command presented Japan with the Potsdam Declaration, which was accompanied by a demand for an unconditional surrender. Japanese government officials considered their response to the proposal and advised the Emperor to accept it, but only if Conditions one to four were agreed upon. Having listened to their advice, the Emperor decided not to surrender. That would prove to be the worst decision he ever made – the Americans detonated two nuclear bombs, over Hiroshima on 6 August and over Nagasaki on 9 August. On 10 August the Japanese Cabinet drafted an 'Imperial Rescript' ending the war, but all Emperor Hirohito seemed concerned about was would he still remain sovereign ruler of Japan.

On 15 August 1945, Emperor Hirohito's recorded surrender speech was played over the radio throughout Japan. Some couldn't believe what they were hearing – it was unthinkable.

One of the main talking points after the war was whether, as Emperor and supreme commander of the Imperial Japanese Army and Navy, Hirohito was directly responsible for the war crimes committed by members of the Imperial Japanese armed forces? For that matter, why wasn't he charged with any crime for the 375 occasions on which he authorised the use of toxic gas during the Battle of Wuhan, China, during the Second Sino-Japanese War of 1938?

However, the reality of how much control he actually had over the decision-making process is definitely debatable. On the other hand, he was fully aware of many of the military decisions which took place during the war, but he simply distanced himself from them through an intermediary.

How culpable he was for the conduct of Japanese forces during the Second World will always be an uncertainty. However, there is no doubt that he should have made the decision to surrender when presented with the opportunity.

CHAPTER TEN

Attack on Pearl Harbor

The attack on Pearl Harbor on the morning of Sunday, 7 December 1941, was one of the most significant events of the Second World War. It marked the beginning of the end for the Japanese Empire. It brought the USA into the war, not only in the Pacific against the Japanese, but in Europe against the Germans, at a time when Britain was struggling to hold back the tide of Nazism.

The Imperial Japanese Empire declared war on both the USA and Great Britain on that Sunday, with both of those nations declaring war on her the following day.

At the time of the attack on Pearl Harbor by the Imperial Japanese Naval Air Service, the United States was still a neutral country.

OK, let's look at the text of the declaration of war by the Japanese on Sunday, 7 December 1941.

IMPERIAL RESCRIPT

We, by the grace of Heaven, Emperor of Japan, seated on the throne occupied by the same dynasty from time immemorial, enjoin upon ye, Our loyal and brave subjects:

We hereby declare war on the United States of America and the British Empire. The men and officers of Our Army and Navy shall do their utmost in prosecuting the war. Our public servants of various departments shall perform faithfully and diligently their respective duties; the entire nation with a united will shall mobilize their total strength so that nothing will miscarry in the attainment of Our war aims.

To ensure the stability of East Asia and to contribute to world peace is the far-sighted policy which was formulated by Our Great Illustrious Imperial Grandsire Emperor Meiji and Our Great Imperial Sire succeeding Him as Emperor Taisho, and which we lay constantly to heart. To cultivate friendship among nations and to enjoy prosperity in common with all nations, has always been the guiding principle of Our Empire's foreign policy. It has been truly unavoidable and far from Our wishes that Our Empire has been brought to cross swords with America and Britain.

More than four years have passed since China, failing to comprehend the true intentions of our Empire, and recklessly courting trouble, disturbed the peace of East Asia and compelled our Empire to take up arms. Although there has been re-established the National Government of China, with which Japan had effected neighbourly intercourse and cooperation, the regime which has survived in Chungking, relying upon American and British protection, still continues its fratricidal opposition. Eager for the realization of their inordinate ambition to dominate the Orient, both America and Britain, giving support to the Chungking regime, have aggravated the disturbances in East Asia. Moreover these two Powers, inducing other countries to follow suit, increased military preparations on all sides of our Empire to challenge Us. They have obstructed by every means our peaceful commerce and finally resorted to a direct severance of economic relations, menacing gravely the existence of our Empire. Patiently have We waited and long have We endured, in the hope that our government might retrieve the situation in peace. But Our adversaries, showing not the least spirit of conciliation, have unduly delayed a settlement; and in the meantime they have intensified the economic and political pressure to compel thereby our Empire to submission. This trend of affairs, would, if left unchecked, not only nullify Our Empire's efforts of many years for the sake of the stabilization of East Asia, but also endanger the very existence of our nation. The situation being such as it is, Our Empire, for its existence and self-defence has no other recourse but to appeal to arms and to crush every obstacle in its path.

The hallowed spirits of Our Imperial Ancestors guarding Us from above, We rely upon the loyalty and courage of our subjects in our confident expectation that the task bequeathed by Our forefathers will be carried forward and that the sources of evil will be speedily eradicated and an enduring peace immutably established in East Asia, preserving thereby the glory of our Empire.

In witness whereof, We have hereunto set Our hand and caused the Grand Seal of the Empire to be affixed at the Imperial Palace, Tokyo, this seventh day of the 12th month of the 15th year of Showa, corresponding to the 2,602nd year from the accession to the throne of Emperor Jimmu.

(Released by the Board of Information, December 8, 1941. Japan Times and Advertiser)

It was interesting to note how Japan viewed matters during those times, although it is unclear if these views were what she actually believed, or were simply her way of justifying her actions. Japan accused both the united States and the British Empire of carrying out 'disruptive actions against the Empire of Japan's foreign policy'. She went on to claim all avenues of discussion for averting war had been exhausted. But at no stage did the Japanese government representatives ever say to their American and British counterparts, 'the talking is over.'

Japan subsequently carried out her invasions of large areas of East Asia for what she called 'the greater East Asia Co-Prosperity Sphere'. This was an Imperialist concept promulgated between 1930 and 1945 supposedly to promote the cultural and economic unity of most of Asia, Australasia, Melanesia, Micronesia and Polynesia.

On 29 June 1940, Hachiro Arita, the Japanese Foreign Minister, announced in a radio broadcast that it was Japan's intention to create a self-sufficient bloc of Asian nations that would be rid of interference or control from Western powers, and that would be led by Japan. That could of course be interpreted to mean that all Japan really wanted was to enjoy the same benefits that America, Britain and Holland had been doing for years.

Japan's attempts at creating her Greater East Asia Co-Prosperity Sphere were already well underway before Japan and the USA had declared war on each other, so much so that in August 1941 the United States imposed embargoes on Japan preventing her from purchasing oil and steel from American companies. It was hoped that this would prevent her continued aggression in Asia and massacres and other violations that Japanese forces were inclined to perpetrate, such as those in Nanking in 1938. These were the hostile and provocative acts Japan used to justify and excuse the attack on Pearl Harbor. However, it is true that at the time of the Pearl Harbor attack, Japan and America actually were in negotiations to prevent such an occurrence taking place.

But the reason behind the attack was more to do with what Japan had planned to do in other parts of the Pacific and Asia. She was in no mood for compromise. Her targeted areas were the American-held territories of the Philippines, Guam, and Wake Island, and the British concerns of Malaya, Singapore and Hong Kong. Pearl Harbor was where the US Pacific Fleet was based, and Japan needed to put that out of action first so that America could not strike back when Japan began her attacks. The attack had to be both quick and effective so as to allow simultaneous attacks to take place throughout South East Asia to provide Japan with raw materials such as oil and rubber.

The attack at Pearl Harbor commenced at 7.48 on a quiet Sunday morning. Three hundred and fifty-three Japanese aircraft, including fighters, dive bombers and torpedo bombers, took part after launching in two waves from six aircraft carriers. All eight US Navy battleships were damaged, four of them sunk. Three cruisers were also lost, three destroyers, an anti-aircraft training vessel, and one minelayer, either sunk or damaged. The Americans also lost a staggering 188 aircraft, most of which didn't even get off the ground. Worst of all, 2,403 Americans were killed in the attack with a further 1,178 wounded. But ground facilities such as fuel and torpedo dumps, a dry dock, a shipyard, maintenance areas, submarine piers, buildings including the intelligence section, were undamaged, which for the Americans was a Godsend.

The Japanese lost 29 aircraft, 5 midget submarines, and 64 of their servicemen were killed. One, Kazuo Sakamaki, was captured.

Sakamaki was one of ten Japanese sailors selected to carry out an attack on Pearl Harbor in a two-man *ko-hyoteki*-class midget submarine on Sunday, 7 December 1941. Of the ten sailors, nine were killed, including the other crewman in Sakamaki's submarine. Sakamaki, who had been chosen for the mission because he had a large number of brothers and sisters, had set an explosive charge to destroy his disabled submarine, which had been trapped on Waimanalo Beach, Oahu. When the explosives failed to go off, Sakamaki swam to the bottom of the submarine to investigate the cause of the failure and passed out due to a lack of oxygen. It is believed that his sub hit coral reefs and sank. Sakamaki was found unconscious on the beach by an American soldier, David Akui, who arrested him and took him into military custody. When Sakamaki regained consciousness, he found himself in hospital under American armed guard. Sakamaki became the first Japanese taken prisoner of war by the USA during the Second World War, and such was the level of bad feeling towards him in Japan that his name was stricken from all Japanese records and he officially ceased to exist; according to them, he should have taken the honourable option and committed suicide. His submarine was captured intact and was later taken on tours across the USA to encourage the general public to purchase war bonds. After he was released from hospital he was taken to Sand Island, an internment camp predominantly for Japanese civilians from the west coast of America. On arrival at the camp, Sakamaki requested that he be allowed to kill himself, but his request was denied. When the war ended, he was repatriated to Japan, by which time he had become a committed pacifist. Sakamaki wrote a memoir about his wartime experiences and spoke at a conference in Texas in 1991 at which he was reunited with the miniature submarine he had sailed in fifty years earlier.

The next few days saw a hive of activity, with declarations of war flying about like confetti. After an urgent sitting of congress on the Monday, America declared war on Japan. Three days later Germany and Italy declared war on America, who later the same day responded with a declaration of war on them. Because Japan had carried out the attack without making any formal declaration of war, Pearl Harbor was deemed to have been a war crime at the Tokyo military trials of 1946-8.

Now I want to look at the two Japanese commanders who directed matters at Pearl Harbor and the parts they played.

Chuichi Nagumo

Nagumo was recognised as a cautious officer who would spend long hours mulling over plans. Some said he was too slow and ponderous to be working in operational roles where events were fluid and changed quickly. The respected Admiral Nishizo Tsukahara was one who wasn't convinced by Nagumo's appointment. He said, 'Nagumo was an officer of the old school, a specialist in torpedo and surface manoeuvres, but he did not have an idea of the capability and potential of naval aviation.'

Nagumo's junior officers looked upon him more as a father figure than a commander.

Nagumo was not in favour of the Pearl Harbor raid but was in charge of the First Air Fleet responsible for the aircraft which attacked the American fleet. The attack was seen universally as a success for the Japanese, but Nagumo was later criticised for not launching a third attack which could have targeted some of the building structures – the fuel storage facilities, the submarine base, an intelligence station and ship repair areas.

After Pearl Harbor, Nagumo commanded the fleet which bombed Darwin on 19 February 1942 in which thirty Allied aircraft were destroyed and eleven ships sunk.

Next he was involved in the Indian Ocean raid on the British Eastern Fleet of 31 March 1942. This cost the British thirty ships sunk and forty aircraft destroyed. Admiral Sir James Somerville had to retreat with what was left of his Fleet to the relative safety of East Africa, having experienced a defeat he would never have believed possible.

By the time of the Battle of Midway, 4 to 7 June 1942, Nagumo's near perfect record and good fortune had run out. The First Air Fleet that he was in charge of took a battering from the US Pacific Fleet. This was almost a payback for Pearl Harbor: Nagumo's First Air Fleet lost four aircraft carriers along with all their maintenance crews and 120 experienced pilots. This was a massive blow for the Imperial Japanese Navy and resulted in them losing the strategic initiative in the Pacific region.

Nagumo was reassigned to the Third Fleet, commanding aircraft carriers in the Guadalcanal campaign after 7 August 1942. His indecision while there led in part to the loss of Japanese vessels which in turn had a marked effect on Japan's overall naval strength in the region.

By 11 November 1942 he had been reassigned to Japan, where he was put in command of the Sasebo Naval District before being transferred to the Kure Naval District on 21 June 1943. Nagumo never seemed to stay in one place for long; whether that was to do with a shortage of senior officers or because he simply wasn't up to the tasks he was being given is unclear.

His next move was to command the First Fleet, where he stayed between October 1943 to February 1944, during which time the fleet was largely involved in training duties rather than operational matters.

As Japan's military situation spiralled towards its eventual defeat, experienced senior Japanese naval officers were at a premium, especially those with battle experience. Nagumo was one such man. On 4 March 1944 he was given command of the 14th Air Fleet and the Central Pacific Fleet stationed in the Mariana Islands. The battle for the Mariana Island of Saipan, which started on 15 June 1944, did not end well for the Japanese. By 9 July they had lost 600 aircraft, 3 fleet carriers, and 29,000 men dead out of a starting figure of 32,000, of whom 5,000 committed suicide.

Nagumo committed suicide on 6 July with a shot to the head in the cave where he was hiding. After his death he was promoted to admiral and awarded the Grand Cordon of the Golden Kite.

Isoroku Yamamoto

When Tojo became Prime Minister of Japan on 18 October 1941, many political observers expected the end of the military career of Yamamoto, but it wasn't to be. Tojo placed him in charge of the Yokosuka Naval Base: 'a nice safe demotion with a big house and no power at all'. But he wasn't there that long. After a new government cabinet was announced, Yamamoto found himself returned to his previous position of power. He had powerful friends, both within the Japanese Royal family and within the Imperial Japanese Navy, where he was well thought of by officers and men alike.

It was as if the future of Japan lay squarely on his shoulders, so much was expected of him. If there was one officer who could lead his men to victory in the war, then it was Yamamoto. It was his plan that was used to attack Pearl Harbor, despite many of his contemporaries having expressed misgivings. But they were all agreed when he said that Japan's hope for victory in the war 'was limited by time and oil'.

They knew all too well the importance of oil. They also knew that if the enemy were able to threaten Japanese merchant shipping, then the Japanese Navy would quickly become obsolete and their war would be over.

Yamamoto wrote in a letter:

> *Should hostilities once break out between Japan and the United States, it would not be enough that we take Guam and the Philippines nor even Hawaii and San Francisco. To make victory certain, we would have to march into Washington and dictate the terms of peace in the White House. I wonder if our politicians who speak so lightly of a Japanese-American war, have confidence as to the final outcome and are prepared to make the necessary sacrifices.*

This was translated in some quarters, especially American ones, to mean that Yamamoto intended to conquer the entire continental USA. In fact it meant the opposite: Yamamoto was counselling caution about becoming embroiled in a war that could cost Japan dearly. Nevertheless, he accepted that a war was coming no matter how he felt about it. All he could do was win battles over the Americans as quickly as possible.

Yamamoto was influential in the development of Japan's land-based naval aviation. He wanted Japanese aircraft to be able to fly longer distances before needing to refuel, and he wanted ones that could carry a torpedo so that when they attacked American shipping the destructive possibilities would be greater. However, although Japan developed long-distance bomber capability, she did not have a long distance fighter escort capability, which meant the bombers were vulnerable to attack from American fighter aircraft on long sorties. When fully fuelled they were particularly vulnerable: the Mitsubishi G3M and G4M medium bombers gained the nickname the 'flying cigarette lighter'. Yamamoto in fact died in a G4M. To address the fighter escort problem, the A6M Zero was developed, with speed and long range.

Yamamoto combined Japan's six largest aircraft carriers into one unit in the shape of the Imperial Japanese Navy's First Air Fleet. This provided a formidable strike force, but it also provided the enemy with a big target to locate and destroy. He did the same for land-based aircraft, organising them into the 11th Air Fleet.

In January 1941, nearly a year before the attack on Pearl Harbor, Yamamoto suggested that Japan revised its plan on how best to attack and deplete the American

Fleet. He pointed out that the plan which Japan had had in place for nearly twenty years had not worked, even during war games. Moreover, America had meanwhile made great advances in the production and technology of naval vessels. Rather than try to gain parity with the Americans by hurriedly building more naval vessels, Yamamoto proposed a pre-emptive strike.

Before such an attack could take place, Yamamoto required the approval of Japan's Naval General Staff, and initially they were reluctant to give it. This was when Yamamoto threatened to resign, gambling on his popularity with the officers and men under his command.

Nagano, Chief of the Imperial Navy General Staff, eventually agreed to Yamamoto's proposal to attack Pearl Harbor, but not to his ensuing battle plans.

After the Pearl Harbor strike, Yamamoto was displeased with Nagumo for two reasons: firstly for not carrying out a third wave attack at Pearl Harbor, secondly for failing to locate the American aircraft carriers that had been out at sea at the time of the attack. But he decided not to publicly reprimand him.

Yamamoto was not just a brilliant tactician and leader of men, he had foresight. In June 1941, when asked by Prime Minister Konoe what he would do if there was a war with the United States, Yamamoto's said, 'I shall run wild considerably for the first six months or a year, but I have utterly no confidence for the second or third years.' If ever a prediction came so readily to fruition, this one did.

There was irony attached to the Pearl Harbor affair. Yamamoto had to almost blackmail his 'bosses' into agreeing to the attack in the first place. But the reality was it was all a waste of time. Why? Because of something the Americans had entitled Plan Orange, a series of war plans written up between the First and Second World Wars by the US Joint Army and Navy Board dealing with a possible war with Japan. In essence, it meant that in the event of a war with Japan, America had no plans to race across the Pacific towards the Philippines.

Yamamoto also did not know that the US Pacific Fleet at Pearl Harbor was not fully manned, and that to get it to wartime readiness would have taken at least six months.

Another thing he was unaware of was the 'Plan Dog Memorandum' written by US Chief of Naval Operations Admiral Harold Stark. This report emphasised that the task of the US Pacific Fleet was only to conduct a defensive war to help Britain and her Allies defeat Nazi Germany. This meant that the United States Pacific Fleet was simply consigned to keeping the Imperial Japanese Navy away from the shipping lanes that led to Australia; any empire-building the Japanese wanted to do apart from that was their own business.

If Japan had not attacked Pearl Harbor, the USA might not have gone to war with Japan at that stage of the war. But Japan did not only attack Pearl Harbor, she also attacked other British and Dutch possessions in the Far East, so perhaps it was always inevitable that the USA would enter the war against Japan in the end.

CHAPTER ELEVEN

Battle of Midway

The Battle of Midway was the turning point of the war in the Pacific, and the beginning of the end for the Japanese. It was a raid on Tokyo by B52 bombers, the 'Doolittle Raid', that got Yamamoto his approval from the Japanese Naval General Staff for his planned operation for Midway Island.

The Doolittle Raid was so named because it was planned and led by Lieutenant Colonel James Doolittle of the US Army Air Force. The idea for the raid came about as a result of a meeting at the White House on 21 December 1941 when Roosevelt informed the Joint Chiefs of Staff that he wanted Japan bombed as soon as possible to boost public morale after the shock attack on Pearl Harbor. As well as being a direct retaliation for Pearl Harbor, the raid was America's way of saying to the Japanese that their country was vulnerable to American air attacks.

Doolittle's first plan was to land the bombers in Vladivostok after the raid and then hand the aircraft over to the Russians as part of Lend-Lease, but Russia had signed a neutrality pact with Japan in April 1941 and could not allow American aircraft to land in her country after bombing targets in Japan. Stalin could not risk provoking Japan in the east while fighting Nazi Germany in the west. In the event, the raiders landed in China. Some of the US airmen were aided by the Bishop of Nancheng Patrick Cleary who was later the Mayor of Cork. In retaliation the Japanese burnt Nancheng to the ground.

The raid, which took place on 18 April 1942, destroyed power plants, a steel mill and oil storage facilities. Eighty-seven Japanese were killed and many more injured. As intended, it proved that America could strike Japan at home. The Japanese diverted considerable resources to defend their mainland and failed to destroy the carrier from which the American planes were launched.

Yamamoto was given the go-ahead to attack the Midway and Aleutian islands and hurriedly began drawing up plans. He sent a force under the command of General Takagi, which included the Fifth Carrier Division, to seize the Tulagi and Guadalcanal islands so they could be used as bases for aircraft. Tulagi and Guadalcanal were both successfully taken.

The Japanese also attempted to take Port Moresby in Papua New Guinea, but failed in what became known as the Battle of the Coral Sea. Although the Japanese managed to sink one American carrier and badly damage another, the Americans managed to badly damage the Imperial Japanese Navy's carrier *Shokaku* and sink the light carrier *Shoho.* The American's also seriously reduced Japanese dive bomber and torpedo aircraft formations.

These ships and their aircraft would be badly missed by the Japanese at the Battle of Midway.

Yamamoto's intention for Midway was to put the US Pacific Fleet, already weakened after Pearl Harbor, out of the war once and for all. His plan was to draw the US Fleet into a trap by sending his Fifth Fleet, consisting of twenty-four ships and vessels, towards the Aleutian islands, raiding the Dutch Harbour on Unalaska Island, and invading the more distant islands of Kiska and Attu.

With the Imperial Japanese Navy's Fifth Fleet attempting to wreak havoc in the Aleutian islands, Yamamoto's First Mobile Force, consisting of twenty-one ships and vessels including four aircraft carriers, was tasked with attacking Midway Atoll and destroying its air force. Once this had been achieved and the Japanese had complete control of the skies, their much larger Second Fleet, consisting of forty-five ships and vessels, would move in and land some 5,000 troops on the beaches of Midway and seize it from the incumbent US Marines.

Yamamoto believed that once the Japanese seized the Atoll, the Americans would immediately send their aircraft carriers to Midway, where the Japanese First Mobile Force would be waiting to destroy them. Then the First and Second Japanese Fleets would finish off the remaining American land forces on Midway.

Yamamoto positioned a line of submarines along the route the American Fleet would take to Midway. Behind this line were elements of the Japanese First Mobile Force and the First and Second Fleets ready to carry out a combined attack. He also had his aircraft reconnoitre

Pearl Harbor and its surrounding area to locate the American carriers.

The opposing sides consisted of the following: the ships of the Imperial Japanese Navy included 4 carriers, 2 light carriers, 11 battleships, 16 cruisers and 46 destroyers, a total of 79 ships. The Americans were able to muster 3 carriers, 8 cruisers and 15 destroyers, a total of only 26 ships. The Japanese had a three to one advantage. The only aspects which drew the two sides a little closer to parity were the number of carrier decks, aircraft and submarines. On paper, Yamamoto held all the cards, and the forthcoming battle appeared a forgone conclusion.

What Yamamoto didn't know, and what was a game changer, was that the Americans knew of the Japanese plans because their code breakers had broken Japanese naval code D (which the Americans referred to as code JN-25). So the commander of the US Pacific Fleet, Admiral Chester Nimitz, was aware of Yamamoto's line of submarines and his reconnaissance of Pearl Harbor. The same intelligence also informed Nimitz that he wasn't as outnumbered as much as he initially believed.

Admiral Nimitz sent his aircraft carriers to Midway earlier than the Japanese expected, hence bypassing both Yamamoto's reconnaissance aircraft and his submarines.

On the first day of the battle, 4 June 1942, Japanese aircraft attacked and damaged the US carrier *Yorktown* so badly that it had to be abandoned. But carrier-based American aircraft then attacked and fatally damaged the four aircraft carriers of Japan's First Mobile Force.

Yamamoto attempted to gather his forces for a landing on Midway, but they were some distance away, and American vessels were too many and too strong.

He took the decision that he could not safely bring his ground troops into play, and aborted the intended invasion of Midway and withdrew.

The Japanese failure at Midway was a major turning point in the Pacific war, changing the balance of power in favour of the Americans. It was a defeat from which the Japanese never fully recovered and marked the beginning of the end for the Imperial Japanese Empire.

As a result of Midway, Yamamoto lost face with his peers, but it was a delicate issue for the senior officers of the Naval General Staff to deal with. Yamamoto remained in place as the commander of the Combined Fleet because to have demoted or moved him would have risked affecting the morale of the officers and men of the entire Combined Fleet. But he was not allowed to make suggestions for any further offensive operations, and instead he had to stick to a prescribed and approved, mainly defensive, naval battle strategy.

Yamamoto found himself involved in a couple of aircraft carrier battles in the Eastern Solomons on 24/25 August 1942 and Santa Cruz Islands on 24/25 September. He further engaged the Americans in several other naval battles around Guadalcanal. Although he managed to inflict losses on the American's Pacific Fleet, he also sustained losses himself, which overall reduced the strength and effectiveness of the Imperial Japanese Navy.

The Japanese were defeated at Guadalcanal and Yamamoto decided to carry out a tour of the South Pacific to inspect his men and their ships. The US Naval Intelligence department intercepted and decrypted a message from the Japanese which outlined in great detail what his movements were to be on this inspection tour. One journey involved him flying from Rabaul to Balalae airfield in the Solomon islands on 18 April 1943. After speaking with Admiral Halsey, Admiral Nimitz authorised a mission to intercept Yamamoto's aircraft and shoot it down. The following day, sixteen Lockheed P-38 Lightning aircraft were sent to shoot down an aircraft with an 'important high ranking enemy officer' on board.

Colleagues of Yamamoto tried to persuade him to cancel the flight, but he went ahead with it. He was on one of two Mitsubishi G4M bomber aircraft escorted by six Mitsubishi A6M Zeroes over Bougainville when one of the American pilots engaged one of the bombers. It was the one Yamamoto was on. The aircraft crashed into the jungle.

The crash site was discovered the following day, along with the dead body of Yamamoto who had sustained two .50 calibre gun-shot wounds, one to the back of his left shoulder, the other which had entered via his lower left jaw and exited above his right eye. All the Japanese civilian population were told was that he had been killed in a plane crash. The Japanese authorities believed that to be told the actual manner of his death would greatly affect the morale of the public.

After 1939 the Germans began sending technical aid to the Japanese. Included was a version of the Enigma machine, called 'Purple'. The British had cracked the Enigma codes long before Pearl Harbor, and American cryptographers likewise built a machine to decode Purple. However, the Japanese were careful never to mention the plan to attack Pearl Harbor, which remained a surprise until the very last minute. There follow three Japanese

messages that were intercepted by American intelligence
in early 1941, clearly showing what they were up to:

Tokyo to Washington.

**Magic intercept Tokyo to Washington #44 – Jan
30, 1941**

Intercept dated January 30, 1941 and noted as
translated 2-7-41 Numbered 44

From: Tokyo (Matsuoka)

To: Washington (Koshi)

(In two parts - complete). (Foreign Office secret).

*(1). Establish an intelligence organ in the
Embassy which will maintain liaison with private
and semi-official intelligence organs (see my
message to Washington number 591 and number
732 from New York to Tokyo, both of last year's
series). With regard to this, we are holding
discussions with the various circles involved at
the present time.*

*(2). The focal point of our investigations shall
be the determination of the total strength of the
U.S. Our investigations shall be divided into three
general classifications: political, economic, and
military, and definite course of action shall be
mapped out.*

*(3). Make a survey of all persons or organizations
which either openly or secretly oppose participation
in the war.*

(4). Make investigations of all antisemitism, communism, movements of Negroes, and labour movements.

(5). Utilization of United States citizens of foreign extraction (other than Japanese), aliens (other than Japanese), communists, Negroes, labour union members, and anti-Semites, in carrying out the investigations described in the preceding paragraph would undoubtedly bear the best results. These men, moreover, should have access to governmental establishments, (laboratories?), governmental organizations of various characters, factories, and transportation facilities.

(6). Utilization of our 'Second Generations' and our resident nationals. (In view of the fact that if there is any slip in this phase, our people in the US will be subjected to considerable persecution, and the utmost caution must be exercised).

(7). In the event of US participation in the war, our intelligence set-up will be moved to Mexico, making that country the nerve centre of our intelligence net. Therefore, will you bear this in mind and in anticipation of such an eventuality, set up facilities for a US-Mexico international intelligence route. This net which will cover Brazil, Argentina, Chile, and Peru will also be centred in Mexico.

(8). We shall cooperate with the German and Italian intelligence organs in the US. This phase has been discussed with the Germans and Italians in Tokyo, and it has been approved.

Please get the details from Secretary Terasaki upon his assuming his duties there. Please send copies to those offices which were on the distribution list of Number 43.

Magic intercept LA to Tokyo Number 067 - May 9, 1941

Intercept dated May 9, 1941 and translated 5-19-41 Numbered 067.

From: Los Angeles (Nakauchi)

To: Tokyo (Gaimudaijin)

(In 2 parts - complete). Strictly Secret.

Re your message number 180 to Washington.

We are doing everything in our power to establish outside contacts in connection with our efforts to gather intelligence material. In this regard, we have decided to make use of white persons and Negroes, through Japanese persons whom we cannot trust completely. It not only would be very difficult to hire United States military experts for this work at present time, but the expenses would be exceedingly high. We shall, furthermore, maintain close connections with the Japanese Association, the Chamber of Commerce, and the newspapers.

With regard to airplane manufacturing plants and other military establishments in other parts, we plan to establish very close relations with various organizations and in strict secrecy have them keep these military establishments under close surveillance. Through such means, we hope to be able to obtain accurate and detailed intelligence reports. We have already established contacts with absolutely reliable Japanese in the San Pedro and San Diego area, who will keep a close watch on all shipments of airplanes and other war materials, and report the amounts and destinations of such shipments.

The same steps have been taken with regards to traffic across the US-Mexico border.

We shall maintain connection with our second generations who are at present in the (US) army, to keep us informed of various developments in the army. We also have connections with our second generations working in airplane plants for intelligence purposes.

With regard to the Navy, we are cooperating with our Naval Attaché's office, and are submitting reports as accurately and speedily as possible.

We are having Nakazawa investigate and summarize information gathered through first-hand and newspaper reports, with regard to military movements, labour disputes, communistic activities and other similar matters. With regard to anti-Jewish movements, we are having investigations made by both prominent Americans and Japanese who are connected with the movie industry which is centred in this area. We have already established connections with very influential Negroes to keep us informed with regard to the Negro movement.

Magic intercept Seattle to Tokyo number 45 - May 11, 1941

Intercept dated May 11, 1941 and translated 6-9-41 Numbered 45.

From: Seattle (Sato)

To: Tokyo

(3 parts - complete)

Re your number 180 to Washington

(1). Political Contacts: we are collecting intelligences revolving around political questions, and also the questions of American participation in the war which has to do with the whole country and this local area.

(2). Economic Contacts: We are using foreign company employees, as well as employees in our own companies here, for the collection of intelligence having to do with economics along the lines of the construction of ships, the number of airplanes produced and their various types, the production of copper, zinc and aluminium, the yield of tin for cans, and lumber. We are now exerting our best efforts toward the acquisition of such intelligences through competent Americans. From an American, whom we contacted recently, we have received a private report on machinists of German origin who are Communists and members

of the labour organizations in the Bremerton Naval Yard and Boeing airplane factory.

(3). Military Contacts: We are securing intelligences concerning the concentration of warships within the Bremerton Naval Yard, information with regard to mercantile shipping and airplane manufacturing, movements of military forces, as well as that which concerns troop manoeuvres. With this as a basis, men are sent into the field who will contact Lieutenant Commander Okada, and such intelligences will be wired to you in accordance with past practice. Kaneko is in charge of this. Recently we have on two occasions made investigations on the spot of various military establishments and concentration points in various areas. For the future we have made arrangements to collect intelligences from second generation Japanese draftees on matters dealing with the troops, as well as troop speech and behaviour.

(4). Contacts with Labour Unions: The local labour unions A.F. of L. and C.I.O. have considerable influence. The (Socialist?) Party maintains an office here (its political sphere of influence extends over twelve zones.) The C.I.O., especially, has been very active here. We have had a first generation Japanese, who is a member of the labour movement and a committee chairman, contact the organizer, and we have received a report, though it is but a résumé, on the use of American members of the Socialist Party. --- Okamaru is in charge of this.

(5). In order to contact Americans of foreign extraction and foreigners, in addition to third parties, for the collection of intelligences with regard to anti-participation organizations and the anti-Jewish movement, we are making use of a second generation Japanese lawyer.

Mitsuo Fuchida

Mitsuo Fuchida was a naval captain and, on Sunday, 7 December 1941, during the attack on Pearl Harbor, he was also a bomber pilot who played an extremely important role on that fateful day. Being part of the first wave of Japanese Nakajima B5N2 torpedo bombers, he had taken off at 6 am, some 250 miles north of Oahu, arriving there at around 7.40 am local time. From there it was a short distance to Pearl Harbor and the United States Pacific Fleet, who were at anchor. Looking out from his aircraft he could see no ground activity below, and the Americans were not firing at him or his colleagues. He pulled back the canopy of his aircraft and fired a blue flare in to the sky. This was the prearranged signal to begin the attack.

Heading down the western coast of Oahu at just after 7.50 am, Fuchida instructed his radio operator, Petty Officer 1st Class Norinobu Mizuki, to send the code word 'Tora, Tora, Tora' to the flagship of the 1st Fleet, the carrier *Akagi*. This meant that the attack had been a complete surprise to the Americans.

Despite being part of the first wave of aircraft that had attacked Pearl Harbor, Fuchida remained there so that he could assess the effectiveness of the attack, and to see in the second wave of Japanese aircraft, only leaving after the second wave had completed their mission.

Safely back to the aircraft carrier, he proudly announced that the United States Pacific Fleet had been destroyed, before turning to inspect his own aircraft, in which he counted twenty-one large flak holes. Fuchida had had a successful day and became a national hero. The Emperor Hirohito was so impressed with him that he granted him a personal audience.

Not only did Fuchida survive the attack on Pearl Harbor, but he survived a similar one on Darwin on 19 February 1942 where he led 188 aircraft into attack. On 5 April the same year he led a series of attacks against Royal Navy bases in Ceylon, the base of the British Eastern Fleet.

On 4 June 1942 Fuchida was aboard the *Akagi* recovering from an emergency appendectomy when the ship was struck by bombs dropped by American aircraft. The bombs started a fire which blocked the ship's bridge, forcing Fuchida and his fellow officers to have to have climb down a rope to the deck. When it came to Fuchida's turn, an explosion blew him off the rope and onto the deck below, breaking both of his ankles. He spent the rest of the war in Japan working as a staff officer.

Fuchida had been in Hiroshima attending a conference with a number of Japanese army officers when he received a phone call from navy headquarters in Tokyo asking him to return, which he did. The day after he left, America dropped the first nuclear bomb on Hiroshima. The next day, he along with a number of other officers were sent to the city to assess the extent of the damage. In those days there was no understanding of the dangers of nuclear fall-out or radiation poisoning to which these men were being exposed by going to Hiroshima. All of the officers in Fuchida's party later died of radiation poisoning, except Fuchida, who displayed no symptoms.

Fuchida was demobilised in November 1945 during the American occupation of Japan. He died near Osaka on 30 May 1976, aged 73.

CHAPTER TWELVE

Territories Occupied by Japan During the Second World War

Part of Japan's unconditional surrender to the Allied powers was an acceptance that, other than the islands which made up the Japanese mainland, control of all the other territories she had occupied during the war was to be divided between the Allied nations. Some of these lands are still in dispute with the countries they were given to at the end of the war.

The Treaty of San Francisco, signed on 8 September 1951 and coming into force on 28 April 1952, was signed by forty-nine nations including Japan. It officially ended the Allied occupation of Japan. It officially saw the end of Japan as an imperial power, but it also saw the return of Japan's full sovereign status. One of its articles stated that Japan accepted the judgements made against her subjects by the International Tribunal for the Far East and the Allied war crimes courts.

The following is a list of colonies, countries or regions that were occupied or annexed by the Empire of Japan up to 1945:

Colonies

Hokkaido – one of the main islands that makes up Japan to this day.

Kuril Islands – a volcanic archipelago consisting of fifty-six islands in Russia's Sakhalin Oblast. Not all of those garrisoned in the Kuril Islands agreed with the surrender of Japan in 1945 and continued the fight against the Russians. But by 4 September 1945 it was all over and Russian forces were in complete control of the islands.

Ryukyu Islands – an island chain that stretches between the south-west tip of Japan and the island of Taiwan. At the end of the Second World War the islands came under American control, but were returned to Japanese control in 1972.

Nanpo Islands – a group of islands located off the south coast of the main islands of Japan. At the end of the Second World War they came under Allied control, but were returned to Japanese control in 1968.

Taiwan – had been ceded to Japan by China in 1895 under the Treaty of Shimonoseki. At the end of the Second World War with Japan's surrender, the island was placed under the control of the Kuomintang-led Republic of China.

Minami-Tori-shima – Also known as Marcus Island, Minami-Tori-shima is a tiny isolated atoll in the Pacific Ocean just big enough to house an airstrip.

The Treaty of San Francisco gave control to the USA. After 1968 Japanese sovereignty was resumed but control of the airstrip remained in American hands. Japan was given control of the whole island in 1993.

South Sakhalin – was a Japanese territory between 1905 and 1945, with North Sakhalin being occupied and under Russian control. After 1945 Soviet Union forces crossed over the islands at the 50th parallel and took control of the entire island.

Kwantung – was a territory that Japan had leased from China as far back as 1905. It was taken over by the Soviet Union in 1945 and they ceded it to China in 1955.

Korea – also known as Japanese Korea, was under Japanese rule from 1910 to 1945. After the Second World War the USA and the Soviet Union divided it along the 38th parallel, but in 1950 war broke out between the north and south divisions. It ended in 1953 but no peace treaty was signed and the two nations are still technically at war to this day. Each claims sovereignty over the other.

Shandong – on the eastern coast of China, was given to Japan after the First World War as part of the Treaty of Versailles, having been a German leasehold since 1897. China objected and, in an agreement brokered by the USA, it came under Chinese control in 1922. With frequently changing borders, it was fought over by Chinese warlords until 1937 when it was invaded by Japan who killed many and destroyed much. The Japanese were driven out by the Kuomintang in 1945, who were themselves defeated by the Chinese communists in 1949. Shandong has been Chinese ever since.

The South Pacific Mandate – consisted of a large number widely-spread Pacific islands including Palau, the Marshalls, the Northern Marianas and several hundred others to the north of Indonesia. After the First World War some were given to the Empire of Japan, others to Australia by League of Nations mandate. Until then they had been part of German New Guinea. After 1947 they were administered by the USA until 1979 after which several of the island groups became independent.

Okinotorishima – is a coral reef that literally consists of two large rocks. Why anybody would go to the lengths of claiming it as a colony is unclear as it looks uninhabitable, but in 1931 Japan did. After Japan's defeat in the Second World War it came under American administration, but in 1968 it was given back to Japan, who thought it important enough to place a 200-mile exclusion zone around it, which is now disputed by China, South Korea and Taiwan.

Manchuria – Japan had occupied Manchuria since 1931. Between 1918 and 1922 she also occupied Primorsky Krai and Siberia in the Soviet Union, east of Manchuria, but she began withdrawing her troops in 1922.

Japan occupied the following nations during the Second World War:

China – with whom she had been at war with since 1931.

Hong Kong – whom she had invaded on 12 December 1941.

Vietnam, **Cambodia**, and **Laos** – which were all invaded by Japanese forces on the same day, 15 July 1940.

Thailand – which was invaded on the morning of Sunday, 8 December 1941, the day after Japan attacked Pearl Harbor in Honolulu.

Malaya, **Sarawak**, **Brunei**, **Labuan**, and **North Borneo** – all were invaded between 27 and 29 March 1942.

Philippines – invaded on 8 May 1942.

Dutch East Indies – previously controlled by the Dutch, invaded by Japanese forces on 18 January 1942.

Singapore – This British Crown property was invaded by Imperial Japanese forces under General Tomoyuki Yamashita on 8 February 1942, and on 15 February 60,000 British and Commonwealth troops under Lieutenant Colonel Arthur Percival surrendered. The Prime Minister described the defeat as 'the worst disaster and largest capitulation in British military history'.

Burma – The Japanese first landed at Victoria Point, the most southernly tip of Burma, on 14 December 1941. On 22 January 1942 they landed in force and began pushing British and Chinese forces out of Burma before occupying the country. They allowed a nominally independent Burmese administrative government, although it was the Japanese who were ultimately in control.

The British Civil Government of Burma, along with a number of Indian civilians, pulled back to Myitkyina in the north of the country. Some

Chinese troops escaped to India, others managed to make their way back to China, chased all the way by Japanese forces.

Occupying Burma gave the Japanese access to the Burma Road, which stretched for over 700 miles and linked Burma with south-west China. It had been built by the British in 1937 by Burmese and Chinese labourers during the Second Sino-Japanese war. Completed in 1938, it was immediately used as a supply route for the Chinese. In July 1940, Britain acceded to a Japanese demand to close down the road and prevent supplies from reaching China. Being able to prevent the flow of supplies along that route was a major motivation for the Empire of Japan to invade and occupy Burma.

East Timor – Portuguese Timor and Dutch Timor were invaded by 1,500 troops of the Imperial Japanese Army's 228th Regimental Group on the night of 19 February 1942. The defenders, 2,000 Allied military personnel from Britain, Australia and the Dutch East Indies, initially put up a stout resistance, but after just a few days most surrendered. The Dutch had lost 300 men, the Australians 150, the Portuguese 75. The British lost five soldiers of the Royal Artillery's, 79th Light Anti-Aircraft Battery.

A few hundred men, mainly Australian commandos, known as the Sparrow Force, continued the fight. Their main tactic was to engage in surprise guerrilla-style raids, striking quickly and retreating before the Japanese had time to organise themselves. These tactics were highly effective and the Japanese suffered very heavy casualties at the hands of the Sparrow Force. As time went on however, the situation worsened for the Australians, even though they were kept supplied by aircraft and ships sailing from Darwin. By the end of 1942 the number of Japanese soldiers on the island had increased to 12,000 and it was becoming harder and harder for the Australians to continue. Between December 1941 and the middle of February 1943, a year after the Japanese had landed, the Australians and remaining Portuguese civilians were evacuated.

New Guinea – The invasion of the New Guinea by the Japanese 8th Army under General Hitoshi Imamura didn't quite go according to plan. It began on 23 January 1942 when Japanese forces captured Rabaul on the north eastern tip of New Britain Island. Over the following year the Japanese turned the area into a military stronghold, building airfields and making Simpson Harbour into a naval base, possibly with the intention of carrying out a full scale invasion of Australia.

However to invade Australia it was first necessary to take Port Moresby. Japan's plan to take Port Moresby came in the shape of the Battle of the Coral Sea, which took place between 4 and 8 May 1942, and was won by the Allies.

The Japanese were in New Guinea for three and a half years, during which it was a constant battle for them and they never had things all their own way.

The Japanese were ultimately defeated by the American blockade which prevented food and medical supplies from reaching them. Because of this 97 per cent of their 127,600 casualties were down to non-combat causes such as disease and malnutrition.

Guam – which was under the protection of the USA, was invaded by Japanese forces on 8 December 1941. It took the Japanese just two days to overcome the American defenders. They stayed in control of the island until the Second Battle of Guam in 1944.

The Governor of Guam, Rear Admiral George Johnson McMillin, was informed about the Japanese attack on Pearl Harbor at 4.45 am on the morning of 8 December, and four hours later Japanese aircraft were attacking the marine barracks and other locations on Guam. During the attack the USS Minesweeper *Penguin* was sunk, and many of the island's main buildings, including the radio station and the Pan American Hotel were damaged or destroyed.

The next day the Japanese attacked again. Some of the previous day's targets were attacked again while some villages and Government House were bombed for the first time. It was an intense day but it was going to get worse. Unbeknown to the defenders, the Japanese had despatched an invasion fleet from Saipan, 137 miles away. The Japanese meant business: the fleet of twenty vessels included four heavy cruisers and four destroyers.

In the early hours of 10 December 1941, 400 Japanese soldiers of the 5th Defence Force came ashore at Dungcas Beach to the north of Agana. The defenders of the Insular Force Guard were quickly overcome and the Japanese made their way in land, dealing swiftly with any resistance. At 4.45 am they had reached the centre of Agana where they were engaged by marines and guardsmen of the Insular Force. Quickly realising that they were heavily outnumbered, Governor McMillin ordered his men to lay down their arms and surrender. By this time the Japanese had landed a further 5,500 men on the island.

After two days of fighting, the American Marines had lost 13 dead and 37 wounded; the Insular Force Guards had lost 4 killed and 22 wounded. In reply, just one of the attacking Japanese force had been killed and six wounded.

The Japanese committed some atrocities in the taking of Guam. One case was the bayoneting to death of Marine Private First Class John Kauffman after the fighting had ceased. Another was that of George Raymond Tweed, a radio operator, who was one of six American seamen who decided not to surrender as instructed. Five were eventually captured by the Japanese and beheaded. Tweed remained at large, managing to do so for two and a half years with help from the local Chamorros. The Japanese tortured and killed some Chamorro people trying to find him but still they did not give him up.

After the murders of his colleagues, Tweed stayed with just one family. He was sheltered by Antonio Artero on his ranch, remaining with the Arteros until the Second Battle of Guam when he was able to signal two destroyers of the US Navy by means of semaphore and mirrors and provide them with intelligence concerning Japanese defensive positions.

Tweed returned to Guam in 1946 to say thank you to the Artero family and others who had helped him during his time in hiding on the island.

Nauru – In 1923 the League of Nations gave Australia a trustee mandate for Nauru, along with the United Kingdom and New Zealand. On 6 and 7 February 1940, two cruisers of the German Navy sank five supply vessels in the waters off Nauru.

There were two reasons that Nauru became of particular interest to the Japanese. They wanted to turn it into a fortress, and they wanted its rich phosphate deposits.

On 26 August 1942, Japanese forces invaded and occupied the island. They built an airfield on it, which became the target of repeated Allied bombing attacks. But on the whole, rather than attack the island the Americans simply decided to bypass it. They did their homework and saw that because of the demanding terrain it really wasn't the type of place they wanted to send ground forces into and risk heavy casualties.

On 25 March 1943 an air raid by the US Army Air Force on Nauru destroyed fifteen Japanese aircraft. At the time there were five Australians there, including Colonel Frederick Royden Chalmers CMG DSO, the Administrator of Nauru, who had been interned on the island. Soon after the air raid, in some warped kind of revenge they were murdered by the Japanese.

The remaining Japanese forces on Nauru, under the command of Hisayuki Soeda, surrendered to Australian and New Zealand forces on 13 September 1945.

After the war at Rabaul in Papua New Guinea an Australian Military court found Lieutenant Hiromi Nakayama of the 43rd Guard Force guilty of the deaths of the five Australians and he was executed by hanging on 10 August 1946.

Wake Island – This coral atoll in the western Pacific was attacked by Japanese forces on 8 December 1941, the same day as the attack at Pearl Harbor. A combination of US Marines, US Naval personnel and a number of civilians, repelled the initial attack, sinking two Japanese destroyers and a transport vessel in the process. The island eventually fell into Japanese hands on 23 December after they returned with a much larger force and the American defenders surrendered. The island remained in the control of the Japanese until they surrendered to the Americans on 4 September 1945.

Attu and Kiska Islands – These islands are part of the Aleutian Islands, which are part of Alaska. Japan invaded them on 6 June 1942. Because of their remoteness and poor weather it took nearly a year for a combined American and Canadian force to go and fight for them, despite the fact that seven years earlier, in 1935, General William Mitchell had told the American Congress that he believed Alaska was the most strategic place in the world and that in the future whoever rules Alaska rules the world.

The islands' strategic value was in being able to control Pacific transportation routes. Both sides recognised their value. The Americans feared the islands would be used by the Japanese to build landing strips from where they could launch aerial attacks on the west coast of America. For their part, the Japanese believed that if they could control the Aleutian islands they could prevent American attacking from across the North Pacific.

Japan's reasons for invading the Aleutians are open to debate, but one thing is clear, the attacks on Kiska on 6 June 1942 and Attu the next day shocked the American people, as it was the first time since the war of 1812, when American forces fought against the British and her Allies, that American soil had been in the hands of a foreign power.

Kiribati – This island group, comprising thirty-two atolls, reef islands and a raised coral island, was invaded and occupied by Japanese forces between December 1941 and 23 November 1943. One of the atolls, Betio, became an airfield and supply base. On 20 November 1943, in an effort to defeat the Japanese forces who had occupied Tarawa Atoll, US Marines carried out an amphibious landing, only to be met by determined Japanese resistance in what history recorded as the Battle of Tarawa. It raged for three days and the Americans won, but at a cost: 1,009 of their men were killed and 2,101 wounded. The US Navy lost 687 men when the escort carrier *Liscome Bay* was sunk. The Americans had thrown 35,000 troops and 18,000 marines into the battle and out of a total of 4,836 soldiers and construction workers, the Japanese lost 4,690 killed. Only 129 construction workers and 17 soldiers survived and were taken prisoner.

Andaman Islands – The British government had used the islands of Andaman and Nicobar in the Bay of Bengal as a penal colony until 1938 for African and Indian political prisoners who were incarcerated in Port Blair's Cellular Jail. On 23 March 1942 Japanese forces invaded the islands. Their main area of interest was the garrison at Port Blair which was home to 300 Sikh Militia under the command of 23 British officers. The men of the militia laid down their weapons and the British officers were sent to a prisoner of war camp in Singapore, possibly Changi.

Japanese forces spent the three years between 1942 and 1945 occupying the Andaman islands. Although official accounts of what took place there during that time have not survived, individual accounts did, and they do not reflect well on the Japanese. Major A.G. Bird, unlike all the other British officers, wasn't sent to a prisoner of war camp in Singapore. He was executed at Port Blair supposedly for being a spy in what can only be described as a horrendous act of cruelty. His legs and arms were twisted until they broke before being beheaded by a Colonel Bucho.

The Commonwealth War Graves Commission website shows an Alfred George Bird who died on 10 April 1942 at Port Blair, although there he is shown as being a civilian. He had clearly lived in the islands for some time as the people of the community affectionately referred to him as 'Chirrie' which means 'Bird' in Hindi.

The worst atrocity carried out by the Japanese while they occupied the islands was the Homfreyganj massacre of 30 January 1944 in which forty-four Indian civilians were shot dead on the premise that they were spies. Many were members of the Indian Independence League, an Indian political organisation which sought the removal of British colonial rule over India, and as such had no direct gripe with Japan, so who they were supposedly spying for is unclear.

During 1945 lack of food was becoming a big problem on the islands. To resolve this issue the Japanese deported several hundred people to an uninhabited island to grow their own food. After the war, Allied naval vessels were sent to the island and the deportation was discovered: only twelve people were found alive.

On 7 October 1945 Major General Tamenori Sato and Vice-Admiral Hara Teizo surrendered the islands to Brigadier J.A. Solomons, commander of the 116th Indian Infantry Brigade, and Mr Noel K. Patterson of the Indian Civil Service.

At a war crimes trial in Singapore on 5-7 March 1946, Sato was found guilty for his part in the capture and murder of a boat load of Burmese civilians while they were trying to flee the islands: 18 men, 9 women and 34 children. Sato was sentenced to death and hung. As for Vice-Admiral Hara, he was arrested by American naval officers, taken to Japan and held at the Sugamo Prison in Tokyo, accused of war crimes. He was put before an American military tribunal on Guam and found guilty, along with other Japanese officers, of 'neglect of duty in connection with violations of the laws of war committed by members of their command'. This related to the execution of US Navy air crews who had been shot down and captured during air raids on Truk. Hara was sentenced to six years imprisonment.

Christmas Island – had been a target for the Japanese since the beginning of the war in South East Asia, in December 1941, because of its rich phosphate deposits which had been mined there since 1899.

A submarine attack in January 1942 followed by air raids in February and March showed Japan's interest. Most of the workers at the phosphate mines and their families were evacuated to Perth, Australia. The island was further attacked by a Japanese naval barrage on 7 March. All that prevented the Japanese forces from walking unopposed onto the island were a British army officer, four NCOs and twenty-seven Indian soldiers. Three days later the Indian soldiers revolted and killed the five British soldiers and imprisoned the remaining civilian workers.

After an air raid on 31 March an unopposed amphibious landing took place by some 850 Japanese soldiers.

When the war ended, seven of the Indian mutineers were tracked down and put on trial at a military court in Singapore. They were found guilty and sentenced to death, later reduced to penal servitude for life.

The territories invaded by the Japanese had a collective population of 460,000,000. In addition, Kohima and Manipur in India, Dornod in Mongolia, and Midway Atoll, part of the USA, all sustained unsuccessful attacks by Japanese forces.

CHAPTER THIRTEEN

Hiroshima and Nagasaki – Atomic Bombs August 1945

Shortly after 8 am on 6 August 1945 an American Superfortress B-29 named *Enola Gay*, flying at 30,000 feet, dropped a single uranium atom bomb named 'Little Boy' with an explosive power of twelve kilotons of TNT over the centre of Hiroshima. Three days later another Superfortress, named *Bockstar*, found its main target at Kokura was obscured by heavy cloud so instead dropped its plutonium atom bomb called 'Fat Man' rated at twenty kilotons over the factory area of Nagasaki.

In Hiroshima more than four square miles of the city were levelled and some 80,000 people, mainly civilians, were killed. In Nagasaki an estimated 40,000 people were killed.

The official numbers quoted could well have been much higher as by this time of the war many Japanese cities were inundated with refugees from other places.

The official estimation for the population of Hiroshima at the time of the attack was 245,000. In addition there were 10,000 Japanese soldiers in the city and 5,000 workers there to make fire breaks, put out fires and clear away rubble. Nagasaki's population was about 260,000.

In Hiroshima, eyewitnesses described a blinding white flash in the sky followed by a rush of air, and then a loud rumble followed by the sound of falling buildings. They also spoke of the darkness which followed as they were enveloped by a cloud of dust.

Before the dropping of the atomic bomb, Hiroshima had been virtually unscathed by Allied air attacks, so any kind of aerial attack was a new experience. The atomic bomb started many fires among the predominantly wooden homes, workshops and other buildings, which burned unchecked for days on end and totally gutted the Old Town.

Despite the death and destruction of the atom bombs, Emperor Hirohito and his government did not immediately surrender. They still wished to continue the war, knowing that tens of thousands of their civilian population had been wiped out in an instant and the likelihood was that if they didn't surrender there would be another such bomb dropped on another Japanese city, and another if they still didn't surrender.

A detailed report of the attack on Nagasaki prepared by the Prefect for the Japanese government on 1 September 1945 said that there had been an air raid alert earlier that day which had been 'relaxed' after which the people of the city went about their usual daily business. The report described the dropping of three parachutes which preceded the blast, the bright flash, the haze of white smoke which quickly darkened, the roaring sound, and a feeling of pressure, wind and heat.

The centre of the damage in Nagasaki was the industrial area between two large Mitsubishi Ordnance

Plants in the Urakami Valley. The harbour and the commercial area escaped with only minor damage, as did the housing in the smaller valley that was screened by a ridge of hills. This was why Nagasaki had fewer killed than Hiroshima, even though the bomb was larger.

After the blast, most citizens tried to leave. Officials and civil defence personnel abandoned their work, not returning until weeks later. This meant that efforts to clear up rubble and debris could not begin until they returned. Most of the dead lay unburied for more than a month after the bombs had been dropped.

The following is taken from a 1946 report by the British Mission to Japan entitled *The Effects of the Atomic Bombs at Hiroshima and Nagasaki*:

> *The effects of an explosion of 20,000 tons of TNT would more than likely cause at a distance of half a mile from the epi-centre of the explosion, an instantaneous pressure rise of about 10 lbs per square inch, falling back to atmospheric pressure in about half of one second, and since during part of this time, there would be a wind in the order of 500 miles per hour, the pressure initially imposed on parts of a building, might be as high as 30 lbs per square inch.*

Most reinforced concrete structures remained structurally undamaged, even close to the centre of the blasts.

In both cities, penetrating radiation resulted in injuries and death, and the medical facilities available to survivors of gamma radiation were of little use.

If Japan hadn't surrendered after the Nagasaki bomb, a third was intended for Kokura, the original target for the second bomb, two weeks later. Its construction, which took place in the Mariana Islands, from where the aircraft for the first two bombs had taken off, was awaiting the main plutonium core to be shipped over from America. If this had not resulted in Japan's surrender, the Americans had a production line of twelve more atom bombs ready for dropping.

The Japanese finally surrendered on 15 August 1945, one day before the Kokura bomb would have been dropped.

CHAPTER FOURTEEN

Japanese War Crimes and Criminals

The political and military leaders of vanquished nations have to suffer being held to account for their actions. Winston Churchill and Arthur 'Bomber' Harris, for example, had to face responsibility for the air raids on Dresden that killed tens of thousands of civilians. Nazi Germany and Japan, however, took war crimes to a whole new level. Japan's particular crime was their treatment of captured soldiers and civilians under her control. The forces of the Empire of Japan were also responsible for numerous war crimes during the Second Sino-Japanese War of 1937 to 1945, and there were other war crimes committed outside this time, but most were carried out during the reign of Emperor Hirohito.

R.J. Rummel in his 1997 book *Statistics of Democide* talks of numbers ranging between 3,056,000 and 10,595,00, 'with a likely mid-total number of 5,964,000', for those murdered by the Japanese between 1937 and 1945. It is important to remember that we are not talking about enemy combatants killed in battle here, but civilians and captured Allied prisoners of war. These figures include those who died of starvation, ill treatment, disease and brutality at the hands of the Japanese.

On 29 April 1946 the International Military Tribunal for the Far East (IMTFE) began the trial of twenty-eight Japanese military and political leaders on fifty-five charges which included waging an aggressive war, murder, and offences committed against Allied prisoners of war and civilian internees.

During the trial the members of the tribunal dismissed 45 of the charges, including all of the murders. The defendants who were found guilty received sentences that ranged from seven years imprisonment to death by hanging. Two of the defendants died during the course of the proceedings. The hearings finally came to an end on 12 November 1948.

The tribunal came about as a result of two meetings that took place between the leading Allied powers before the end of the war. One was the Cairo Conference of 27 November 1943 which resulted in the Cairo Declaration. It included the following text:

> *The several military missions have agreed upon future military operations against Japan. The Three Great Allies expressed their resolve to bring unrelenting pressure against their brutal enemies by sea, land, and air. This pressure is already rising.*
>
> *The three Great Allies are fighting this war to restrain and punish the aggression of Japan. They covet no gain for themselves and have no thought of territorial expansion. It is their purpose that*

Japan shall be stripped of all the islands in the Pacific which she has seized or occupied since the beginning of the First World War in 1914, and that all the territories Japan has stolen from the Chinese, such as Manchuria, Formosa, and the Pescadores, shall be restored to the Republic of China. Japan will also be expelled from all other territories which she has taken by violence and greed. The aforesaid three great powers, mindful of the enslavement of the People of Korea, are determined in due course Korea shall become free and independent.

The second was the Potsdam Conference of 26 July 1945 which resulted in the Potsdam Declaration. The declaration determined the following:

- *The elimination for all time of the authority and influence of those who have deceived and misled the people of Japan in to embarking on world conquest.*
- *The occupation of points in Japanese territory to be designated by the Allies.*
- *That Japanese sovereignty shall be limited to the islands of Honshu, Hokkaido, Kyushu, Shikoku, and such minor islands as we determine.*
- *That the Japanese military forces, after being completely disarmed, shall be permitted to return to their homes with the opportunity to lead peaceful and productive lives.*
- *That we do not intend that the Japanese shall be enslaved as a race or destroyed as a nation, but stern justice shall be meted out to all war criminals,*

including those who have visited cruelties upon our prisoners.

• *The Japanese government shall remove all obstacles to the revival and strengthening of democratic tendencies among the Japanese people. Freedom of speech, religion, and of thought, as well as respect for the fundamental human rights shall be established.*

• *Japan shall be permitted to maintain such industries as will sustain her economy and permit the exaction of just reparations in kind, but not those which would enable her to rearm for war. To this end, access to, as distinguished from control of, raw materials shall be permitted. Eventually Japanese participation in world trade relations shall be permitted.*

• *The occupying forces of the Allies shall be withdrawn from Japan as soon as these objectives have been accomplished and there has been established, in accordance with the freely expressed will of the Japanese people, a peacefully inclined and responsible government.*

• *We call upon the government of Japan to proclaim now the unconditional surrender of all Japanese armed forces, and to provide proper and adequate assurances of their good faith in such action. The alternative for Japan is prompt and utter destruction.*

The Potsdam Declaration was issued five weeks before Japan officially surrendered on 2 September 1945 and eleven days before the atom bomb was dropped on Hiroshima. Emperor Hirohito announced to his people his acceptance of the terms of the declaration on 15 August 1945. His announcement, played over the radio, was a recording that had been made two days earlier. It was translated in to English and broadcast overseas to Allied nations at the same time:

To our Good and Loyal Subjects.

After pondering deeply the general trends of the world and the actual conditions obtaining in our Empire today, we have decided to effect a settlement of the present situation by resorting to an extraordinary measure.

We have ordered our government to communicate to the governments of the United States, Great Britain, China and the Soviet Union that our Empire accepts the provisions of their joint declaration.

To strive for the common prosperity and happiness of all nations as well as the security and wellbeing of our subjects is the solemn obligation which has been handed down by our imperial ancestors and which lies close to our heart.

Indeed, we declared war on America and Britain out of our sincere desire to ensure Japan's self-preservation and the stabilization of East Asia, it being far from our thought either to infringe upon the sovereignty of other nations or to embark upon territorial aggrandizement (to increase the power or Reputation).

But now the war has lasted nearly four years. Despite the best that has been done by everyone, the gallant fighting of the military and naval forces, the diligence and assiduity of our servants of the state, and the devoted service of our one hundred million people, the war situation has developed not necessarily to Japan's advantage, while the general trends of the world have all turned against her interest.

Moreover, the enemy has begun to employ a new and most cruel bomb, the power of which to do damage is indeed incalculable, taking the toll of many innocent lives. Should we continue to fight, not only would it result in an ultimate collapse and obliteration of the Japanese nation, but also it would lead to the total extinction of human civilisation.

Such being the case, how are we to save the millions of our subjects. Or to atone ourselves before the hallowed spirits of our imperial ancestors? This is the reason why we have ordered the acceptance of the provisions of the joint declaration of the powers.

We cannot but express the deepest sense of regret to our Allied nations of East Asia, who have consistently cooperated with the Empire towards the emancipation of East Asia. The thought of those officers and men as well as others who have fallen in the fields of battle, those who died at their posts of duty, or those who met with untimely death and all their bereaved families, pains the heart, night and day...

The hardships and sufferings to which our nation is to be subjected hereafter will certainly be great. We are keenly aware of the inmost feelings of all of you, our subjects. However, it is according to the dictates of time and fate that we have resolved to pave the way for a grand peace for all the generations to come by enduring the unendurable and suffering what is unsufferable...

Let the entire nation continue as one family from generation to generation, ever firm in its faith in the imperishability of its sacred land, and mindful of its heavy burden of responsibility, and of the long road before it.

Unite your total strength, to be devoted to construction for the future. Cultivate the ways of rectitude, foster nobility of spirit, and work with resolution, so that you may enhance the innate glory of the imperial state and keep pace with the progress of the world.

The announcement of the Japanese surrender nearly didn't take place because several officers of the Japanese Army believed that to ever surrender was dishonourable to the point of being unthinkable. When they became aware of the existence of the recording, one thousand officers and men of the Imperial Japanese Army launched an attack on the Imperial Palace in Tokyo the evening before the day of the intended announcement. They made their way inside the palace but had no idea where the recorded speech was stored or who had it. Despite their best efforts they failed to locate it and the official Japanese surrender was announced as planned the following day.

The Allied nations could not agree how the trials would work or who would be tried. So Supreme Commander of the Allied Powers General Douglas MacArthur took control. He ordered the arrests of thirty-nine suspects, most of whom were members of Japan's war cabinet, which was led by **General Tojo**. When American soldiers went to Tojo's home to arrest him, he attempted to commit suicide by shooting himself in the chest, but he survived. He remained conscious and was recorded saying:

> *I am very sorry it is taking me so long to die. The Greater East Asia War was justified and righteous. I am very sorry for the nation and all the races of the Greater Asiatic powers. I wait for the righteous judgment of history. I wished to commit suicide but sometimes that fails.*

Tojo was found guilty of 'waging wars of aggression, war in violation of international law; unprovoked or aggressive war against various nations; and ordering, authorising and permitting inhumane treatment of prisoners of war'. At his trial Tojo said, 'It is natural that I should bear entire responsibility for the war in general, and needless to say, I am prepared to do so.' He apologised for the atrocities committed by those under his command and begged the USA to treat the Japanese people with compassion. Tojo was found guilty of all charges and sentenced to death. He was hung at Sugamo Prison on 23 December 1948.

There follows a short selection of the principal Japanese war criminals who were convicted at the IMTFE:

Shumei Okawa was a nationalist and writer. He was prosecuted as a Class A war criminal, with the offences of joint conspiracy to start and wage war, conventional war crimes, and crimes against humanity. Okawa was the only one of the defendants who was neither a member of the government nor the military, but he had long been agitating for war between Japan and the West, an allegation he denied. During his trial it was noted that his behaviour had started to become erratic. His trial was stopped to find out what was wrong with him. US Army psychiatrist David Jaffe examined Okawa and declared that in his opinion he was mentally unfit to stand trial. The President of the Tokyo Tribunal, William Webb, was left with no option but to drop all charges against him. Whether he was actually mentally ill or simply feigning madness remains open to debate. He was transferred to a US Army hospital in Japan where it was determined that his mental instability could have been a result of syphilis. He was transferred to the Tokyo Metropolitan Matsuzawa Mental Hospital where he remained until 1948, after which he lived a free man until his death in 1957.

Matsuoka Yosuke was Minister of Foreign Affairs between 1940 and 1941. He had lived in the USA between 1893 and 1902 and graduated from the University of Oregon Law School in 1900. He died of natural causes in Sugamo prison on 26 June 1946 while awaiting trial for war crimes.

Admiral of the Fleet **Nagano Osami** also died of natural causes during the trial. He was arrested by American forces in September 1945 and charged with Class A war crimes. He was the last Fleet Admiral of the Imperial Japanese Navy and died of pneumonia on 5 January 1947.

General Kenji Doihara was chief of the Japanese Army's military intelligence services in Manchukuo. He was heavily involved in the trade of heroin and opium, which he helped to spread throughout China for his personal gain as well as that of the authorities in Tokyo. This was achieved by setting up health centres throughout the country under the pretence that people would be injected to prevent the spread of tuberculosis which was rife at the time. But the medicines contained opium, which turned millions of unsuspecting patients into opium addicts. He was also involved in assassinations, opium dens, blackmail, gambling houses, extortion, and bribery. Prostitution was another big money maker for him: he forced tens of thousands of Russian white émigrés to work in a network of brothels. He was tried, found guilty of war crimes, and hung in December 1948.

Koki Hirota was Prime Minister of Japan between 1936 and 1937. He was found guilty of waging wars of aggression in violation of international law, waging unprovoked war against the Republic of China, and disregard for duty to prevent breaches of the laws of war. He was hung in 1948.

He was accused, as Foreign Minister, of receiving regular reports of the atrocities that members of the Imperial Japanese Army had carried out, and doing nothing about them. Hirota's sentence was deemed by many to have been excessive as he had no authority over those who had carried out these atrocities.

General Seishiro Itagaki had served with the Imperial Japanese Army since 1904 and between 1938 and 1939 had been Minister of War. During the war he was commander-in-chief of the army in Korea, until 1945 when he was stationed in Singapore and Malaya. He was the representative who surrendered Japanese forces to

Mountbatten in Singapore on 12 September 1945. Soon after this he was arrested by the Allied authorities and charged with war crimes, specifically in connection to the Japanese invasion of Manchuria when he was Minister of War, and for allowing the inhumane treatment of Allied prisoners of war during his term as commander of Japanese forces in South East Asia. He was found guilty and hung on 23 December 1948 at Sugamo Prison.

General Heitaro Kimura was commander of the Burma Area Army between August 1944 and September 1946. He too was arrested after the war and charged with war crimes, which for him was connected to the Burma Railway. Although it was built between 1942 and 1943, and Kimura did not arrive in Burma until late 1944, he was still charged with the abuse and deaths of the Allied prisoners of war and civilians who had been used to construct the railroad. He was hung in December 1948.

Lieutenant General Akira Muto led troops during some of the worst excesses of the Nanking Massacre in China. At the time of Pearl Harbor he was serving as director of the Military Affairs Bureau and was believed to have been one of those who planned the attack. In April 1942 he was appointed commander of the Second Imperial Guards Division at Singapore, two months after the Japanese had captured the island from British and Commonwealth forces. In June 1944, he found himself on the move again, when he was transferred to Sumatra, and three months later was transferred to the Philippines where he became chief of staff to General Tomoyuki Yamashita. He was accused of being responsible for conducting a campaign of torture, slaughter and numerous other atrocities there against the Filipino civilian population, Allied prisoners of war and civilian internees. He was arrested after the war, found guilty of war crimes, and hung at Sugamo on 23 December 1948.

General Iwane Matsui was commander of the force sent to China in 1937 which was responsible for the Nanking Massacre. There is some controversy over the conviction of Matsui. In delivering their verdict on 12 November 1948, the tribunal made the following observations:

> *The Tribunal is satisfied that Matsui knew what was happening. He did nothing, or nothing effective to abate these horrors. He did issue orders before the capture of the city enjoining propriety of conduct upon his troops and later he issued further orders to the same purport. These orders were of no effect, as is now known, and he must have known. He was in command of the Army responsible for these happenings. He knew of them. He had the power, as he had the duty, to control his troops and to protect the unfortunate citizens of Nanking. He must be held criminally responsible for his failure to discharge this duty.*

Most of the massacres occurred in the first few days after Japanese soldiers arrived in Nanking on 13 December 1937. Matsui did not arrive in the city until four days later. In the days leading up to his arrival, he had been stricken with malaria. Matsui's conviction was one of the first examples of an individual being held responsible for a group action, known as 'command responsibility'.

Prince Yasuhiko Asaka, on the other hand, didn't face any charges. He was the son-in-law of Emperor Meiji, and by marriage was also the uncle of the Emperor Hirohito. In December 1937 he was the ground commander of the Japanese forces involved in the final assault at Nanking, but despite all of the crimes and atrocities carried out by men under his direct command, he never faced any charges.

In November 1937 Asaka was under the command of General Matsui. When Matsui fell ill, Prince Asaka took over and was in temporary command of the final assault on Nanking on 2-6 December.

The Allied authorities did not wish to prosecute, let alone execute, members of the Japanese royal family. To have done so might have led to a resurgence of Japanese aggression against the Allies. General MacArthur granted them immunity from prosecution.

Hirohito ratified a directive on 5 August 1937 which removed the constraints of international law on the treatment of Chinese prisoners of war by Japanese soldiers. So the Emperor himself bore much of the responsibility for the atrocities at Nanking.

Out of eighty senior officers who were recalled from China after the Nanking Massacre, only Matsui was singled out for criticism.

Somebody high up in command had to take the blame for the atrocities that were carried out at Nanking. It wasn't going to be Emperor Hirohito, and it wasn't likely to be Prince Asaka, so that just left one individual to take the blame, General Matsui. Matsui was a scapegoat.

After the war most of the Japanese Royal family, including Asaka and his family, lost their royal status and became commoners. His mansion in Shirokanedai was taken away from him and he and his son were prevented from holding any political or public office. After the war he spent most of his time playing golf. He died of natural causes on 12 April 1981, aged 93.

Fearing a possible backlash from the Japanese people, General MacArthur banned photography of the hangings at Sugamo, despite being requested to do so by President Truman to allow it. Many of the death sentences were commuted to prison sentences. In 1950 MacArthur ordered the reduction of some prison sentences and directed that all those on life sentences would be released on parole after fifteen years.

Why wasn't Emperor Hirohito charged with War Crimes?

At an Imperial conference on 1 December 1941, Hirohito approved attacks against the United States, the British Empire, and the Dutch colonial empire. He had clearly been guilty of waging an aggressive war.

It would appear that General MacArthur, Brigadier General Bonner Fellers, and their staff, wished to exonerate Emperor Hirohito and all members of the Japanese royal family from blame for the atrocities that Japanese forces had carried out during the Second World War.

According to Shuichi Mizota, the interpreter for Admiral Mitsumasa Yonai of the Imperial Japanese Navy, Fellers met with Yonai at his office on 6 March 1946 and told him, 'It would be most convenient if the Japanese side could prove to us that the Emperor is completely blameless. I think the forthcoming trials offer the best opportunity to do that. Tojo in particular should be made to bear all responsibility at this trial.'

General Tojo said at his trial that Emperor Hirohito was the ultimate authority responsible for Japan's actions during the war, but he was later persuaded by Major General Ryukichi Tanaka to change his testimony so as to remove all reference to the Emperor.

CHAPTER FIFTEEN

Compensation

In October 2000, Tony Blair's Labour government announced that it had agreed a multi-million pound compensation deal with former British military personnel who had been held as prisoners of war by the Japanese during the Second World War. The compensation, £10,000 per veteran, or their surviving spouse, was in recognition of the 'appalling' experiences many of them had to endure during their time in captivity. Those in line for a payment numbered some 16,700. Although it had taken British politicians fifty years, and most had died in the intervening years, it was on the whole well received by veterans.

In 1999 British government ministers ruled out the idea of seeking additional money from the Japanese government under the 1951 San Francisco peace treaty. It anyway provided former PoWs with only £76 each.

Direct applications by British veterans to the Japanese government for compensation, along with an apology, had previously been turned down by the courts in Japan.

The first of the compensation cheques was sent out by the War Pensions Agency on 1 February 2001. By then it was estimated that ten veterans were dying each week, which meant that between the time the government first made the announcement of the payments in October 2000 and the first payments being sent out, approximately 150 veterans had died.

Eamonn Fingleton, in an article dated 3 May 2006, calculates that Japan has paid out a total of $1 billion in post-war compensation while Germany has paid out $70 billion, and that Japan had three times as many victims as did the Germans. He also points out that in the first six years after the war, America paid Japan $2 billion in aid.

Conclusion

The beginning of the Imperial Japanese Empire and the reign of Emperor Meiji in 1868 saw a massive shift in Japanese society away from the feudal system ruled by the Tokugawa Shogunate military government that had prevailed since 1600. By the time of Emperor Meiji's death in 1912, Japan had gone through a remarkable transformation, both politically and economically. It had changed from being a predominantly agricultural country split into 250 semi-autonomous areas to a united nation that was an industrial superpower on the world stage.

During the Meiji era, Japan looked to Britain and the west for an example of what she strived to be, but somewhere between the wars she changed direction, possibly because of the way she was treated at the Paris Peace Conference of 1919. The Peace Conference did not give her the recognition she felt was her due for the assistance she afforded the Allies in the First World War. Her reaction was to show the western world that Japan was not a second class nation but a major power in her own right. The path that she chose was war, and in doing so woefully underestimated the power of the USA and the western Allies. This led to the destruction of her empire.

After the war, Japan embraced pacifism – Article 9 of the Japanese Constitution outlaws the use of war as a means to settle international disputes. Instead of war, she directed her energies towards industry and became one of the world's richest nations. The war saw a once great empire utterly defeated – a just punishment for her unwarranted aggression and her disgraceful treatment of defenceless civilians and prisoners of war.

Sources

Herbert, Edwin, *Small Wars and Skirmishes: 1902-1918 – Early Twentieth-century Colonial Campaigns in Africa, Asia and the Americas* (Foundry, 2003).

Miller, Harry and Harper, R.W.E., *Singapore Mutiny* (OUP, 1984)

Rummel, R.J., *Statistics of Democide* (LIT Verlag 1997).

ibibilio.org

thedailybeast.com

britishnewspaperarchive.co.uk

ussr.fandom.com

The Author

Stephen is a happily retired police officer having served with Essex Police as a constable for thirty years between 1983 and 2013. He is married to Tanya who is also his best friend.

Both his sons, Luke and Ross, were members of the armed forces, collectively serving five tours of Afghanistan between 2008 and 2013. Both were injured on their first tour. This led to his first book; *Two Sons in a Warzone – Afghanistan: The True Story of a Fathers Conflict* (2010).

He also has a teenage daughter, Aimee. Both of his grandfathers served in and survived the First World War, one with the Royal Irish Rifles, the other in the Mercantile Navy. His father was a member of the Royal Army Ordnance Corp during and after the Second World War.

Stephen collaborated with Ken Porter on a previous book, *German POW Camp 266 – Langdon Hills* (2012). It spent six weeks as the number one best-selling book in Waterstones, Basildon, in March/April 2013. They have also collaborated on four books in the 'Towns & Cities in the Great War' series by Pen & Sword, and Stephen has written other titles for the same series: *The Surrender of Singapore – Three Years of Hell 1942-45* (2017); *Against All Odds: Walter Tull the Black Lieutenant* (2018); *Animals in the Great War* (2018); and *A History of the Royal Hospital Chelsea 1682-2017 – The Warriors Repose* (2019). The last two were written with his wife, Tanya.

Stephen has co-written three crime thrillers, published between 2010 and 2012, centring round a fictional detective named Terry Danvers.

When he is not writing, Tanya and he enjoy the simplicity of going out for a coffee, and walking their four German Shepherd dogs early each morning when most sensible people are still fast asleep in their beds.

Index